About T

Colleen Townsend Evan~ ~ ~ ~ ~
many others) was a promising young Hollywood actress
in the late 1940s who met Christ and handsome Louis
Evans about the same time. Eventually, she gave up her
career and in 1950 married Louie, casting her in the new
role of pastor's wife, which she has enjoyed now for
these many years. The mother of four grown children
(one finishing college, the others in grad school), Coke
is actively involved in the congregation her husband
serves and in an inner-city ministry in Washington,
D.C., as well as on several boards of national organiza-
tions. Coke has written many other books (by various
publishers), including these that are available today:

> *Give Us This Day Our Daily Bread*
> *Love Is an Everyday Thing*
> *Teaching Your Child to Pray*
> *The Vine Life*
> *A Deeper Joy*

Louis H. Evans, Jr. ("Louie" to Coke and many others)
attended San Francisco Theological Seminary and The
University of Edinburgh. He has served congregations
in Bel Air and La Jolla, California, and is now Senior
Pastor of The National Presbyterian Church in Washington, D.C. Louie and Coke are boldly committed to each
other in marriage and yearn for others to share the
concept of commitment, a key to a really satisfying marriage. And that's the reason for this book. Louie has also
written another book, *Covenant to Care*, published by
Victor Books.

B O L D
COMMITMENT

Colleen &
Louis Evans, Jr.

While this book is designed for your personal
enjoyment and profit, it is also intended for
group study. For use in group study, obtain
the accompanying Leader's Guide with Victor
Multiuse Transparency Masters from your lo-
cal bookstore or the publisher.

VICTOR

BOOKS a division of SP Publications, Inc.
WHEATON, ILLINOIS 60187

Offices also in
Whitby, Ontario, Canada
Amersham-on-the-Hill, Bucks, England

Unless otherwise noted, Scripture references are from the *Revised Standard Version* (RSV). Other quotations are from the *King James Version* (KJV); and *The New Testament in Modern English* by J. B. Phillips (PH), © 1958, The Macmillan Company. All quotations used by permission.

Cover photo by David C. Maas

Recommended Dewey Decimal Classification: 173
    Suggested Subject Heading: MARRIAGE

Library of Congress Catalog Card Number: 82-062943
ISBN: 0-88207-284-6

VICTOR BOOKS
A division of SP Publications, Inc.
P.O. Box 1825 ● Wheaton, Illinois 60187

CONTENTS

GRATEFULLY...

Through the years there have been so many people who have touched our lives and influenced our thinking, and we would like to give them all credit for anything of value we have borrowed, made part of our lives, and now share here. But our "rememberers" aren't that good! So to those who have lectured at conferences we have attended, written books we have read, and whose ideas we have absorbed to the point where we don't know where theirs stop and ours begin—*thank you!*

We also are very grateful to our friends who have shared both the joys and honest struggles of their marriages. They have added so much to our lives and to the writing of this book.

Our thanks also to some special people who have exercised their gifts of helps and given us the practical aid we needed to see this project through to fruition: Jayne Crawford for her typing and Jeanine and Gene Arnold for a quiet, loving atmosphere in which to work.

"This Is a Book of Hope"
Preface

No two people are alike—no two marriages are alike.
God's creation is full of exciting diversity, especially
when it comes to people. Within His creative guidelines,
there is room for this diversity; He honors it, and so do
we. Therefore, this is a book of hope, but not a book
pushing a neat little formula that will work in some
magical way for every marriage. There will be no sure-
fire answers for all the couples of the world, no "pink
pill" approach to successful marriage. Rather, we would
like to look with you at some biblical premises in light
of our contemporary scene. What, for instance, is the na-
ture of authority and the real meaning of submission?
We intend to dig deeply into the liberating love of Jesus
Christ, the designer of marriage, as we come to grips
with some of the problems every marriage has to face.
We consider the exciting interdependence of persons
and the roles of husband and wife, not as they are predetermined solely by sex or tradition, but as they are seen
through the New Testament prism of the gifts of the
Spirit. We look at some of the basics of a good marriage.
We also share some steps in the sometimes painful yet
liberating process of communication.

At first we considered doing this book as a dialogue,
but we found that to be a very difficult form for us. We
then moved on to the idea of a monologue—two persons' ideas presented as one voice—but that was both
contrived and awkward for us. Finally, with the help of
a few close friends, we decided that the most natural
way would be for each of us to write certain chapters,

choosing the areas for which our individual gifts equip us and where we feel most at home.

We have no illusions about our ability to do justice to this vast subject of marriage. We already feel the frustration of not being able to deal with certain areas in depth, and we are keenly aware of the many aspects of life together we are leaving completely untouched, either because of our own limitations or the limitations of time and space. However, our prayer is that in the simplicity of what is shared here, there will be a ministry to some. We see marriage as the most exciting and fulfilling of all human relationships. It is also demanding for it cuts to the core of our selfish, hedonistic "me first" contemporary society. Marriage is the most practical arena of self-discovery, the most basic building block of any society. Far more than a loving, supportive relationship, marriage unites two human beings with everything that is theirs. It invites them to contribute whatever they are—all that they are—to a new style of life. Marriage enables a man and a woman to give each other the gift of themselves in a bold, courageous, lifelong commitment. For us this is exciting, and through this book we dare to commend such a commitment to you.

1 Marriage: Convenience or Commitment?

by Louie

The train for New York was filling up fast. I found an empty seat beside a young woman. She was in her late twenties, attractive and well dressed. We began to talk, sharing our mutual sorrow over the dumping grounds of America as our train rolled past acres of junked cars, city trash heaps, and strewn backyards. We found we had similar concerns in a number of areas. As the miles clickety-clacked away and our conversation continued, I found the young woman to be surprisingly open about her personal life, specifically her relationship with her boyfriend. He wanted her to live with him, but she wasn't sure she would and she wasn't sure she wouldn't. "I'm definitely not ready for marriage," she said emphatically, "and maybe I never will be."

"What do you feel about marriage?" I asked.

"What do *you* feel about it?" she asked, pointing to my wedding ring.

"I'm sold on it," I answered. "But, as with any relationship worth its salt, it has to be worked at. Good marriages don't just happen—and even the best marriages have problems that need to be worked out."

"Why stick with it, then?" she asked, looking some

11

what pensively at a fold she was adjusting in her skirt. I had a feeling we had touched on a sensitive point. "If there is any kind of hassle or inconvenience in a relationship, why stick around?"

I shared with her for a while the deep satisfaction of a committed relationship as opposed to the popular trend of "checking out" when things get tense. I tried to be honest about some of the hang-ups I had brought into my marriage, about the mixture of love and honesty from my wife, Colleen, that I felt characterized the covenant we have together. I explained how Christ had been a great therapist in our relationship, stripping back the layers of pride I had carefully maintained and adding new styles of openness in which I could communicate my need instead of continuing in my old pattern of self-sufficiency. I told her how Christ had given Colleen, who was raised in a home without a father, the strength and security she needed to emerge as a whole person. I said we felt it took two whole people, secure enough to risk growing and changing together, to make a good marriage. I talked a bit about our kids—about the terrific joy they had brought into our lives and about some of the honest encounters we had had with them. I guess I got pretty excited, because she looked straight at me and smiled. "You're *really* turned on by marriage, aren't you?" she said.

"Does it show?" I laughed.

"Sure it does, but I like it. You really find it fulfilling?"

"Tremendously!"

"Well, you're one of the few persons I've met who feels that way. You give me hope, but it sure has to work against the odds." Then she told me about her folks' divorce, which had been a source of great pain in her life. She also had a number of friends who had tried marriage and were opting out.

"Not very good data, is it?" I queried.

"No, but I wish it were."

The train began to slow down. We were coming to her station. She stood up and took her bag from the rack above. Then, with a warm yet wistful look, she tossed me a parting word. "Take care of the good thing you've got going."

I fumbled for a card in my wallet and handed it to her. A smile crossed her face. "A preacher . . . wouldn't you know!" she quipped.

"But marriage is not just for preachers," I called out just before she was beyond earshot.

I think I understand what had soured that young woman on marriage. She was like so many other young people I had counseled. They were painfully disappointed with family life as they had known it. They wanted no part of the Standard American Package—the money, the big cars, the house with the oversized mortgage, the pressures, and finally the legal hassles of divorce. I imagine my young friend had been given "everything"—except time, attention, and a viable model of a warm, real and loving relationship. Now she was saying, "*This* is marriage? Not for me!"

But I felt I heard her saying something more: "I wish it were different. I'd like to believe in marriage, but I just can't believe in the ones I've seen."

The train jolted forward and we were on our way once again. Alone with my thoughts, I found myself wondering again what goes wrong with so many commitments that start out with such hope?

Is she, and the host of others who share her feelings, being "turned off" by marriages that have given in to the ease of a convenience society, the escape exits of contract relationships, and the staggering changes that are molding our society by sheer pressure?

Convenience Relationships

Convenience has become a key word in our culture. And

thank God for many of the conveniences. But tragically convenience has also become a hallmark of our relationships: "I'll stand by you—as long as it is convenient. But if things get tough, don't expect me to stay around. You're gentle on my mind." That kind of attitude is devastating to the human personality. When one person feels the other might opt out of the relationship as soon as things become inconvenient, their very foundations are shaken.

Each of us longs to share life with someone who will brave all barriers to stand by us, and for whom we will do the same. We long to love—and be loved—unconditionally, without the fear that inhibits our behavior when we feel we are "on trial." The truth is, marriage cannot be simulated; living together is not marriage. True marriage is the boldest human commitment possible. It says, "I'll be with you through it all ... the "better" and "the worse"! That is *security!*

But when two people merely play at marriage, or lower their marriage to a contract spelling out performance and expectancy, there is the danger of "small print" of which only one of the partners is aware. Then, when the honeymoon is over and real life with its joy and struggle settles in, the one partner may move away from the hassle of any pain with the simple accusation: "You have broken the contract." And the relationship is aborted.

"But I didn't know," comes the anguished cry of the other, who didn't understand the "small print" which might have said, "You be the successful provider, and I will love you always. But fail, and it's all over." Or, "Be the beautiful healthy entertainer for my business contacts, and I will forever take good care of your needs. But once you show dissatisfaction with the meaningless chatter of cocktail parties—or if you become ill and unable to function as my hostess—we're finished."

For some people, "I love you" means "I love me, and

it makes me feel good to have you . . . as long as you
don't inconvenience me."

I don't remember where I first read this definition of
love, but the message it conveys I cannot forget. In fact,
it haunts me as I witness the shocking decline of lasting
marriages, both in our society and in the smaller circle
of those we know and love. It seems to me those who
hold this view of love and marriage are half-hearted
lovers who, consciously or unconsciously, design their
relationships with fire escapes; then rush for the exit at
the first smell of smoke.

It is strange that a few years ago couples who were
experimenting with new lifestyles and living arrange-
ments that very often mocked marriage were considered
to be the bold, adventurous ones in society. Now I have
a growing conviction that the reverse is true. Those who
are ready to give themselves to *one* person in an unre-
served, lifelong commitment are the courageous, real
adventurers in life.

In his excellent book, *Saying Yes to Marriage*, William
H. Williman speaks of the riskiness of linking your life
to one other human being from this day forward, accepting all their strengths and weaknesses for better and for
worse, and asking them to do the same for you. At the
same time he affirms the fact that it is wonderful, exciting, and possible to do, for this is the commitment the
Christian is asked to make, and God never asks the
impossible. As we give ourselves and receive another,
He is there to enable it all to be.

Williman goes on to talk about the riskiness of lifelong commitment which makes marriage unpopular
with many. Perhaps we need to look at some of the
reasons this is particularly so in our society today.

In his provocative book, *Future Shock*, Alvin Toffler
calls us the "throw-away society." At one point in the
book the idea of different marriage partners for different
stages of a fast-changing life was discussed (Random

House, pp. 47-67). The results of a study done by pollster Daniel Yankelovich give support to the extent of Toffler's "throw-away society" theory. The study which focused on family attitudes indicated that nearly half of America's younger families put freedom over authority, and duty to self over duty to others—even marriage partners and children (*The American Family Report: Raising Children in a Changing Society*, General Mills, Inc.). If true, this is where much of the struggle with commitment lies today, for built into the very heart of commitment is the concept of endurance. How can endurance be accepted and embraced as a positive characteristic in a "throw-away society"?

Commitment

What does commitment look like? If we were to take it apart, what would we find? Most certainly one of the first things we would discover is that it has a price. The person making a lifelong commitment agrees to both physical and mental fidelity, which means they give up their right to "option tending." This, of course, is more costly to some than to others. Those influenced and shaped by the "me" generation often unconsciously expect closeness without being willing to share themselves. They may want intimacy without the cost of taking risks. It just isn't possible. There is so much talk about wanting to be "free"; yet we know there is no *true* freedom while refusing to be accountable to the one we say we love.

In making a commitment we must be prepared to pay the price. But we can also expect to receive beyond measure, for as two people give themselves to one another, without keeping an eye on those exit signs to run for at the first smell of smoke, they set in motion an exciting process of self-discovery.

William H. Williman says: "A person is shaped by his or her decisions and how he or she stands by them. Our abiding commitments make us who we are and give us unified characters in place of a tangled mass of loosely connected instincts, whims, and fads. Like the Christian faith itself, marriage requires basic commitment which is willing to endure times of stress, to renew and persevere together" (*Saying Yes to Marriage*, Judson Press, p. 71).

Earlier we said that built into the very heart of commitment is the concept of endurance, and now we see that endurance has its own inherent rewards. For there is a kind of personal growth that does *not* take place unless we are willing to build upon our past. This means perservering in our most important human relationship rather than running for the exit and giving up at any sign of strain and stress. Then as a couple begins to grow, to lean into their relationship in this way, they make a most exciting discovery. What has been believed and hoped about Christian marriage is true! Every aspect of life together—communication, intimacy, love, appreciation, sex—will grow and come to its full potential, but only in the arena of this *unconditional commitment!*

"Commitment, like the amaryllis, if allowed to endure, will bloom again and again."

I wish I knew whom to thank for those words. They express so well what we have experienced.

Over 30 years ago, following God and the desire of our hearts, Coke (my nickname for Colleen) and I made a lifelong "no-exit" commitment to one another. As we began our marriage, I think we both felt we knew just about all there was to know about our new mate. However, it couldn't have been more than two or three weeks after the wedding when we began to discover how far from the truth our knowledge was. In that short time of experiencing life's most intimate human relationship, we saw how little we really knew of the one we married, or of ourselves. Then began a process we continue to this day—one of discovery, risking, and sharing, and finally trusting—knowing that whatever vulnerable new area we expose to the other will not bring rejection. As we have done this through the years, the roots of our relationship have gone deeper and deeper into the soil of God's love. The process has forced new growth in both our lives, and brought a level of depth and freshness to our relationship that has surprised us with joy. But it hasn't been easy. Sometimes the self-exposure has been painful and has taken weeks, months, and sometimes years to work through. Even the happy sharing of a dream, or a newly discovered gift or talent, has demanded energy as it is uncovered and encouraged by a nurturing spouse. But always the process of hanging in there and building upon our past has caused our basic commitment, like the amaryllis, to bloom again and again.

Another aspect of commitment is covenant, modeled after God's unconditional covenant with us. He never turns away from us, His children, just because we disappoint Him. He comes back to us again and again, often with honest encounter, but always with untiring covenant love. As I see it, the epitome of this love is Jesus, who was God's act of love toward a hostile world. Nothing could drive Him from His covenant; His commitment was firm. No degree of inconvenience and no broken agreements could suppress the flow of His love.

A covenant says, "My commitment is to you as a person, not to the roles you fulfill for my need or satisfaction. There is nothing you can say or do that will ever make me stop loving you."

All of us yearn for this kind of bold commitment from the human being most important to us. Without it, we just never become the people we were meant to be. Without commitment, we also exhibit an interesting psychological response. Wanting something so basic—yet being frustrated in finding it—we begin to fear the very thing we long for, or we try to rationalize it away. Perhaps this is why some people are turning away from the covenant of marriage to new philosophies and convenience relationships. Add to this the massive changes in our society in recent years, and the lack of authentic, attractive models for lasting relationships, and it's no wonder there is confusion about the institution of marriage.

And yet the search goes on. According to a National Institute of Mental Health survey, 87 percent of the college students polled listed family life as one of their most important goals. It seems it isn't marriage as a relationship that is in question but the *quality* of the marriage itself. People are hungry for more fulfilling and deeper relationships in marriage. They are beginning to define marriage as two people who love and like each other, who can have fun together, who can share life's highest goals—sharing a deep and genuine companionship—and who can consciously make a lifelong commitment to each other and to each other's growth as persons. A new generation—and many of us in the middle and older generations as well—wants something more than an empty traditional definition of marriage.

Colleen and I do, and we do feel there *is* more. Marriage has a thrilling potential that can be realized by those who are willing to stretch and grow through their commitment to each other and through the process of openness and honesty in their life together. There is much of the old that is worth rediscovering, although admittedly some of the traditional must be challenged. All around us are new discoveries waiting to be incorporated into marriage to make it a richer experience.

Covenants are costly, yet enormously rewarding. A *bold commitment* requires sacrifice, but how exciting to discover that, in keeping with the way God created us, that very sacrifice is part of our fulfillment.

2 God First:
He Makes It Possible

by Coke

Anyone who really knows me knows how deeply I feel about marriage. When I try to put words around my feelings, I fumble—and often, get so choked up I'm unable to speak at all. Friends laugh at me. But it's true. After thirty years of marriage to Louie, I am still filled with a sense of wonder and gratitude for the life we share. *But* having said that, I need to say something more.

Marriage, no matter *how* good, is not the answer to life. *God is.*

So often we expect a husband or a wife to be in our life what only God can be, and the burden is too great. It is so important to the health of a marriage that neither partner expects the other to provide all their emotional support. No person can make another person happy. My happiness is my responsibility, my choice, daily.

A good friend of ours who has just gone through a painful break with his wife keeps saying: "She expected me to be everything to her, and there just wasn't *enough* of me to meet her needs." Our deepest needs are *not* to be solved in this way. Marriage is not God, and no person can give us that for which our heart most desperately longs. The only way that deepest void is filled is when we become united with God in Jesus Christ. The number one spot in every heart is meant for Him, and things just don't function well when we insist on putting someone else in His place. Rather, there is deep truth in the concept that until we love God more than our husband or wife, we will never know how freely and deeply we *can* love the one with whom we have made a life covenant. When the love of God in Christ invades us, we are able to take His gift of love and love our mates—and others—in a way surprising even to ourselves. "We love, because He first loved us" (1 John 4:19). He shows us how—in His total commitment to us, His radical, unconditional love, even to death.

Christ Provides Security

When God comes first in a marriage, something happens for which I personally am very grateful. I know there is something more than my relationship with Louie on which I can depend. As important as my marriage is to me, I need to know there is more. Our individual relationships with Christ give it a basis of support so that our marriage doesn't have to carry all its own weight. We are not a closed system without any help from the outside. So many couples seem to live only for each other and, when something threatens their relationship, there is no one to help. How much better it is, when differences and problems arise, for two people to go to God. As they come closer to Him, their reference point, they find themselves closer to one another. I know. We've been there, and it works. It isn't that I always have to accept Louie's position, or that he has to bow to mine. When we both seek God in a situation, there is often a third, more creative, answer to the difference we have. The bonus is that as two people *both* submit to Christ—and to one another out of reverence for Him—

there is something above and beyond that guarantees their love for each other. This is the best security base I know for any marriage—not our outer circumstances or our theology of marriage—but our relationships with Him! *Christ* is our security. He is also our great "constant" in life.

Today, as I was standing at the washing machine, stuffing it with dirty clothes, I realized that just a few days earlier I had been standing in the same spot doing the same thing—but my feelings were at an entirely different place. I had been strangely discouraged; I can't remember why. My *feelings* were undependable. At that earlier moment I was so lacking in confidence I could not imagine how Louis could possibly have been so dumb as to choose me for his wife. Silly, perhaps, but that is what my feelings told me. I remember sighing and thinking, *Well, Lord, You're in charge around here. . . . I'm tired (which, come to think of it, may have been my problem) so please take over my feelings, because I know these are not from You.*

Well, today it was a different story. I was rested, my feelings were behaving, and I even wondered if Louie knew how lucky he was to have me for his wife. In fact, I could hardly wait for him to come home so that I could ask him.

Our feelings can vary from day to day. A close friend who has one of the greatest marriages I know shared with me a feeling she had very early in their married life. One day, without reason or warning, she looked at her husband and her heart sank. Something had happened to her feeling for him. It was gone. She was conscious of saying to herself, *OK, this is it. This is the way it's going to be. I've made a commitment to my husband—and to God—and I'm going to live by that commitment, not my feelings.* And so she proceeded by faith to love her husband, sincerely if not with the same sense of thrill and depth of emotional feeling. It wasn't long before one day, just as suddenly as the feeling had gone, the feeling returned . . . and more! It overflowed! Her love for her husband was renewed.

In the years that have followed, her feelings have known the ebb and flow—the highs and the lows—of a creative personal life. But her love—their love—has grown steadily, and their marriage has been a *joy*, not only for them but for anyone who knows them well. She learned that just as we can't live the Christian life on feelings alone, neither can we judge our marriage by a feeling of the moment. Our feelings are fickle and often unreliable. But God is a great stabilizer, a great constant in our lives—and in our life together.

Christ Our Therapist

He is also the great therapist for a husband and wife. We all come into marriage with hang-ups: mistaken ideas, the myth of perfection, and the need to grow. We have to resist the urge to remold our mate, and we must open ourselves instead to the work of God in our own life. One of the most difficult lessons for me has been learning that I am responsible for *my* life, not Louie's. Each day I *choose* either to respond to God and His ways, or to resist His work in me. No one can do this for me, nor can I assume this responsibility for another.

Therapy begins the moment I honestly pray, "Make *me* the person I should be in my marriage." When I think of all the areas of my life God has had to work on since I first prayed that prayer, I am amazed at His patience and faithfulness. Beginning with the basic security I needed to be able to give myself away in a lifelong covenant, God has again and again provided the resources I needed for emotional growth and freedom. And the work goes on. There isn't a day in my life when I don't need my liberator-therapist. Marriage can help in this process. It is a splendid forum for growth, but it cannot ultimately free us. That is God's work.

Christ Our Provider

God is also the great provider of our material needs. I remember feeling such confidence during the early part of our marriage when we were in seminary. We were always short of money, yet we were certain that God would provide what we actually needed. And He did! There was a time when we were totally out of cash to live on for two weeks. We had eaten everything edible in the cupboard, and I had given Louie the last of our food for lunch. I still remember it was a hard-boiled egg and a glass of tomato juice. Poor Louis started mumbling about taking me away from a career with a good income only to drag me off to seminary and starvation. We laugh about it now, but Louie says at the time he felt painfully inadequate. I remember how we knelt in the tiny living room of our basement apartment and prayed for resources. Later in the day, Louie took a break from his studies to check the mail and found a letter from a church where he had preached six weeks earlier. He had not expected any payment from it, but there it was, $40! It was a sign from the Lord that He would provide—and He always has. Things have been tight much of the time, but there has always been enough for the important things—the right things—and enough to share with others.

There have been a few times when our desires have gotten out of hand, and God has always drawn us back to the simpler life that is right for us. I think of the house we bought some years ago in California. It was a nice house with a lovely, big yard and a gorgeous view of the ocean. It was a bit too much for us to handle, perhaps, but it was pretty. However, it took only a few months for that "too much" to weigh us down financially, and we couldn't wait to sell that house and get back to something more basic. The little home that took its place was right—just as the row house in Washington, D.C. is right for *this* season of our lives.

Christ Forgives and Heals

Another great thing Christ does in a marriage is to forgive and heal. A marriage is closer to being genuinely Christian at its core, not when it is free of all difficulties, but when both partners are open to the work of God in their lives. There is no perfect marriage, no marriage that does not need God's forgiving ways as part of its everyday lifestyle. In this atmosphere two people can feel forgiven by God and so be generous in forgiving one another. In this atmosphere healing takes place, and love and growth walk hand in hand. It is a beautiful thing to see a couple allow God to release His grace and power in their lives at the very point of their need.

I know it has been said repeatedly, but I don't think it can be said *too* often: *Marriage is work.* And forgiveness, both the giving and receiving, is an essential part of that work.

I'm an idealist but I have a deep conviction that there is no relationship too far gone for Christ to make it new. He can heal any hurt, restore lost hope, renew love. But, of course, there is a condition—it requires *two* willing people to make the miracle work.

Amy and Peter were marvelous people. Both of them were intelligent, attractive, warm human beings. They had been married for over twenty years, had four lively children, and from the outside things looked great. But on the inside their life together had turned sour. They both worked at consuming jobs, had little time together, and began to feel like strangers with each other. With their communication system out, they were gradually drawn to other people. At first, it was just someone to talk to over lunch, someone to listen. But as their needs grew, the "only a friend" plot thickened, and the time came when they had to face the fact that they were in trouble.

Stories like this usually end up in the divorce court, but not so in this case. In a real sense it was only the beginning because Amy and Peter had all the makings for a miracle. They both loved God, and down deep they wanted their marriage to work, so they were open to help. They sought a counselor who shared their faith, and he took them through a long and painful journey of discovery and insight. He finally urged them to take the hurts—and all that needed forgiving—to Christ, the only One who can really handle such things.

I know they were frightened at this point. I still remember the tremble in Amy's voice when she asked me to pray for them as they took that step together by faith. What if it didn't work? But as they yielded themselves to Christ for His forgiveness and healing, the miracle of Christian marriage happened, as it will when two people seek the will of Christ. Following the forgiveness and healing such a new commitment was born in their hearts in the months that followed that they felt they wanted to be remarried.

Because they had never divorced, they couldn't be remarried, but with their minister's help they designed a simple service of reuniting them. On a lovely Sunday afternoon their children stood up with them as they rededicated their lives to Christ—and to each other. I was there as part of their extended family that day, and believe me, there wasn't a dry eye in the church. Your marriage may not need the major reuniting my friends needed, but every marriage needs reuniting in some way every day.

And every marriage needs healing—for there is no way to love and share life's *most* intimate human relationship without knowing pain and hurt.

A scene that took place years ago crosses my mind and becomes part of my life again. Hazel, a beautiful woman in her late twenties, was standing at our door saying good night after a meeting in our home. A gentle breeze blowing through the open door brought the summer scents of gardenia and jasmine to us. As we stood laughing and talking, the light from the lamp on the porch caught Hazel in its glow. I remember thinking how attractive she was—inside and out—and then the next thought followed predictably: "A good catch for some fortunate man."

At that moment our youngest son, who had apparently heard us and climbed out of his crib to join the fun, toddled up to me and nuzzled his head against my body lovingly. I picked him up and balanced him on one hip while his body curled naturally against mine. I continued talking to Hazel until I noticed tears in her eyes. She was staring at Jamie, and said, after what seemed like a very long time, "It must be wonderful to have a family!"

"Oh, it is!" I replied. "Hectic sometimes, but wonderful." And then I'm afraid I was insensitive to her feelings as I blurted out:

"But you'll know that for yourself one day—that is, I'd be surprised if you didn't!"

At that, fear crossed her face, and she said, "No . . . never. I'll never get married, never have a family. I couldn't take the pain that comes with loving that much." With that she turned abruptly and walked out of the light into the darkness of the street.

Now I know marriage is not for everyone. There are some very right reasons for some people deciding not to marry, but fear of intimacy and pain is not one of them.

Hazel, you're right, I thought. *Love, and your heart will be broken—not once, but many times. Pain is an inherent part of love. But, Hazel, on a deeper level you are wrong, for you've failed to remember that God is a healer. He promises to be part of the covenant relationship you make when you marry. Because love is tender, you will hurt and be hurt. There will be pain. But He will be there to heal the hurt and to set you on your way stronger than before. Say no to love and you are saying no to life. Rather—trust God, and live. For He is the great healer and forgiver—in things both great and small.*

I agree with Lloyd Ogilvie's observation, "We are far too timid in sharing the secret of Christian marriage. It is a Christ-healed, spirit-filled relationship" (from material presented at Continental Congress on the Family, St. Louis, 1975).

Christ is the One who provides love, security, patience, stability, forgiveness, healing—every resource we need for a great marriage. Then lifelong union is possible, not because we are great lovers, but because God, in *His* greatness, has unlimited ability to help us *be* and *do* what He originally designed for us in marriage. Our confidence is in Him, so we can make—and keep—life's boldest human commitment. As husbands and wives we were never meant to go it alone. God waits to do for us what we cannot do for ourselves. With Him at the center of our lives and marriages, the possibilities are more exciting and beautiful than our highest dreams.

He makes it possible—and you know who He is.

3 Mutual Submission: Who's in Charge Here?

by Louie

There is a lot of pain in many marriages—much of it rooted in the problem of authority.

Kirk was a strong individual, highly creative and well known in business circles. His wife, Carolyn, was a gifted person, energetic, efficient, imaginative, and one to throw herself with all her might into anything she did. But she didn't have much opportunity to exercise her strengths. To say that Kirk was difficult to live with would be an understatement. He was bossy, demanding, not always ethical, and often insensitive to other people's feelings—especially to Carolyn's. He took it for granted that she would go along with him without question.

Some years ago Carolyn told me she had to make a decision. She had tried to have an honest, open discussion with her husband, but he couldn't handle it. He interpreted her concern over his behavior as criticism and went into a rage. It was her complete approval and absolute acquiescence he demanded, nothing less. So Carolyn had to decide between ending the marriage by exercising her strengths—or yielding in every way to her husband. She chose to yield.

Carolyn realized she had a limited number of choices. She could go through the war of separation and divorce—and war it would be—leaving emotional, financial, and spiritual devastation in its wake. Or she could submit to Kirk's pathologies, learning to deal with his tirades and self-centeredness, and hoping that some day Kirk might change.

In choosing to submit to her partner she was giving up the ideal of an open, honest, and shared life. Instead, she would have to bite her tongue, swallow her pride, and put a lot of her creative abilities into cold storage. But that was the only way she saw of saving their marriage. Carolyn had bought a kind of peace.

Some forms of peace are not as creative as others. In Carolyn's case it meant the loss of some outstanding human potential; and yet all was not lost. Some of the time Kirk was a delight—alive, interesting, jovial, even thoughtful, and certainly never a bore! There were compensations, and Carolyn chose to live with them. It was her choice, and I won't fault her for that!

But Carolyn's decision was not without its costs. Part of the strain she bore was evident in painful migraines. As years went on, her three children carried scars that caused serious trouble. That was a big price to pay for peace.

If Carolyn had chosen the first alternative, that of divorce, she would have refused to submit, and there would have been a rupture in the relationship. Perhaps the cause would have been tagged "immaturity," "an inability to deal with frustration," a "lack of communications skills and ways of dealing with anger," or maybe it would have been described as an escape from a demeaning, destructive partnership. Whatever the label, the experience would have been painful.

The second alternative meant submitting to another's weakness and living with pain, but keeping the marriage together. In making her choice Carolyn followed what she felt was the biblical view of submitting to one's husband in all circumstances. Paul said, "Wives, be subject to your husbands, as to the Lord. For the husband is the head of the wife as Christ is the head of the church. . . . As the church is subject to Christ, so let wives also be subject in everything to their husbands" (Eph. 5:22-24). Peter said the same thing: "Likewise you wives, be submissive to your husbands, so that some, though they do not obey the word, may be won without a word by the behavior of their wives" (1 Peter 3:1).

The Pharisees of Jesus' day would have agreed with Carolyn. They took God's curse on woman seriously: "To the woman He said, 'I will greatly multiply your pain in childbearing; in pain you shall bring forth children, yet your desire shall be for your husband, and he shall rule over you'" (Gen. 3:16).

In the Jewish culture of the New Testament a woman was definitely a second-rate citizen. Sons inherited land, but daughters received only maintenance. If a wife found anything, it belonged to her husband, as did the work of her hands. Even a woman's inheritance, should there be no male to receive it, could be used by her husband for his desires. A woman was not given a teaching position among the laity in the synagogue. If she had a question, she could ask her husband when they got home. The cultural conditioning was so deep it is not surprising that it found expression in the teaching of the New Testament writers themselves.

But let us take a second look at the biblical material. It appears there are four phases to humanity in Christ: (1) Created potential and parity, (2) the Fall, (3) re-creation in Christ, and (4) glorification. I will not get into the last, except to say that any Christian who is aware of the promise of Christ and believes it, looks forward to that day of Christ's triumphal return. At this point, however, I want us to focus our attention only on the first three phases.

Potential

The first was the state of innocence in which man and woman were created with a kind of parity. God created mankind male and female. "And God blessed *them*, and God said to *them*, 'Be fruitful and multiply, and fill the earth and subdue it'" (Gen. 1:28, author's italics). Evidently the potential for dominion was given to both male and female. When God created woman, He created her as helper (in the Hebrew, *azar*) to man. But this word *azar* does not imply inferiority or second-rate status. God Himself is *azar* to man, "A very present help in trouble" (Ps. 46:1). If anything, the word indicates man's incompleteness without woman—his need for her— even as man is incomplete without a relationship with God. Likewise, woman needs man. So close is the need factor that when man was presented with woman, he cried out, "Bone of my bone, and flesh of my flesh" (Gen. 2:23). His very joy was an expression of his need for her. In this phase of humanity, male and female became one flesh. The two were one, not alike, and the difference was good. They shared a unity of need and complementation in parity.

Fall

In the second phase of humanity, that of the Fall, all of life came under the curse of sin. The relationship of man and woman was affected in that man became the ruler of woman and the parity was ended. The wife from that time on was subject to the authority of her husband. The earth was subject to the futility of mankind's distorted rule that became demonic and rapacious. Man himself was cursed to wrest his living from a thistle-filled and thorn-bearing earth (Gen. 3:16-19). We must remember that all the Old Testament was written during this phase of the Fall and the curse. It was during this phase that Pharisaism was born and developed, with all its legal rules and burdens that Christ described as heavy bur-

dens placed on people's backs which the Pharisees
would not lift a finger to lighten (Matt. 23:4). Christ was
angered by the insensitivity and judgmental attitude
that pointed a finger at outward behavior without at-
tempting to understand the inward need of the individual. It was that burdensome legalism that drew Paul's
sharpest criticism—that the law could not give life or
liberate souls oppressed by the curse.

New Relationships

Thank God, we are not stuck in the mire of this second
phase. In Christ we have moved on to the third phase of
humanity. Through His death and victorious resurrection we have been set free from the curse. In Him we
are made new creatures! Here, in this third phase, the
image of God's original design is replacing the old forms
of legalism and subjugation. "The old has passed away,
behold, the new has come" (2 Cor. 5:17). Old inferior-
ities are eliminated; woman has again become the helper, the peer of man. "There is neither male nor female;
for you are all one in Christ Jesus. And if you are
Christ's, then you are Abraham's offspring, heirs according to promise" (Gal. 3:28-29). Former lords have become servants after the example of Christ striving to
bring everyone to maturity in Christ (Col. 1:28). Husbands now are to give up their lives for their wives as
Christ gave up His life for the church, that they might
be presented before Him "in splendor," the splendor of
full maturity. The subjugations once operating under the
law are now removed. Man's subjugation to the law,
woman's subjugation to man, human subjugation to
death, are now replaced by all of humanity's subjugation
to Jesus Christ. Every man, woman, and child has direct
access to Jesus Christ through the Holy Spirit. And
through the same Spirit, Jesus Christ has access to the
mind and will of every person. Therefore, if anyone
puts any other relationship ahead of that to Jesus Christ,

he or she is not worthy of Christ (Matt. 10:34-39).

Instead of lordships that hold others in inferior positions, those who have experienced Christ's redemption are called to a life of service. Now, as Christians, we submit to one another out of reverence for Christ, for His example of servanthood, His liberating death and resurrection, and out of reverence for the gifts that His Holy Spirit creates in each believer. Submission is a biblical quality of life that should be operating in all of us as we relate to others.

The Christian wife submits herself to her husband. My wife submits to me in a hundred different ways! But that is not all. I also submit to her. The concept of submission was never meant for only one person in a relationship. The Spirit calls us to a mutual submission. "Be subject to *one another* out of reverence for Christ" (Eph. 5:21, author's italics) is the key verse here, and *mutual submission* is the overall theme of the verses that follow. A wife is to submit to her husband "as to the Lord" (Eph. 5:22), but that does not mean that her husband *is* her lord. She is to serve her husband in the line of serving Christ. (The Greek word meaning "as" indicates intention, the intention of a wife to serve her husband as he attempts to achieve his dominion over some part of God's creation—just as she serves Christ and the realization of His kingdom).

Compare Ephesians 5:22 with its parallel passage, Colossians 3:18. "Wives, be subject to your husbands, as is fitting [proper] in the Lord." This means to us that wives are to please the Lord primarily—and then they are to submit to their husbands as the husbands labor for the Lord's kingdom. A Christian wife will submit whatever resources she has to undergird her husband in his efforts to complete Christ's ministry. She will go with him where he feels God is leading him to work, because he is probably the chief breadwinner. She submits to the valid demands made upon her because of the scheduling involved in his work; she makes the way straight for his endeavors. She is indeed his "helper," someone he needs for his completion, just as he needs the Lord and His resources.

If, however, the husband demands something that is outside the will of Christ and requires the wife to give up those things that belong to Christ or to others, then his wife is under no obligation to obey her husband if in so doing she must disobey Christ, her Lord (1 Peter 4:1-5). Any husband who makes such demands on his wife simply demonstrates his foolishness and misplaced ego.

Some Christian teachers insist that a woman should go along with *anything* her husband asks because he is her "lord." Sadly, there is much heartache because of this narrow and incorrect interpretation of Paul's injunction which can be a reflection of a male ego that has refused to be conformed to loving as Christ loved. After listening to some of the things such husbands demand of their wives—whether in scheduling priorities or in sexual activities—I am convinced that a wife only reinforces her husband's arrogance and demeans herself by submitting to him. Nobody wins by such appeasement. The wife who goes along with a husband's desire when she feels it is contrary to Christ denies her Lord and permits her husband to stumble headlong into a pit of error.

We understand that many wives during the Watergate debacle were in the dark as to their husbands' activities. But one wife, discovering what her husband was involved in, blew the whistle by calling upon him to act in a moral way. He did! He withdrew from the questionable activities and was not caught in the whirlpool of misdeeds.

I know that if I am bound on a course that Colleen feels will be less than God's best, believe me, I am going to hear about it! I love her for that. If she were to submit to me in such a way as to lessen her clarity of commitment to Christ, I would be very unhappy. I deeply believe that God's will is the best thing that can happen to us. Often Coke is the instrument of challenge through which I become aware of God's will for my life. I am grateful, even though it may—and sometimes does—sting my male pride. But God forbid that a man never allow his wife to dialogue or disagree with him. If he does, he knows little of mutual submission. We have seen more marriages blessed because a woman "by her chaste and reverent behavior" was not only loyal to her husband in chastity, but reverent to Christ in obedience, than by a woman who submitted so much that she covered her Christian witness and denied her Lord.

When the question comes up, "Who's in charge here?" the Christian wife should be able to say, clearly and boldly, "Jesus Christ."

A few years ago, when I was considering a call to another church, Colleen exercised a strong influence on my decision. She confronted me, mildly but firmly, because she thought I was not open to the new situation. (I wasn't. I had five good reasons why I shouldn't go!) Finally she said, "Honey, I just don't think you're open-minded about the matter!"

At first I smarted under the confrontation, but she jarred me loose from a "dead center" position. We agreed that I should go away for a few days and pray. On my return, I was "in neutral gear," willing to go or willing to stay. In this attitude we went to the new city, preaching in a nearby church, and met with the committee for a long afternoon of openness and candor that I doubt would have been possible if I either had desperately wanted the position or had been close-minded about it. We looked at it as honestly as we could. When the call came, I accepted it. The decision was mine and I knew Colleen would go along with whatever I decided—once I had given open consideration to it. But we talked and prayed it over so thoroughly that our minds had a common response when the voice on the other end of the phone said, "It is the unanimous decision of the committee...." I felt good about letting my wife influence my life. Her sensitivity and gift of discernment were much-needed elements. If I had been hardheaded about it, I could have denied her challenge and missed God's direction. In that case, there would have been grave doubts about the quality of my leadership. Jesus Christ is her Lord, not I, and when she submits to His lordship, I am blessed.

Yes, husbands also submit to their wives, loving them "as Christ loved the church and gave Himself up for her, that He might sanctify her" (Eph. 5:25-26). To me this passage means that Christ loves the church, and that He gives Himself to the church to bring her to her full potential, in the splendor of her maturity, free of anything that would hold her back from the full realization of God's design. In doing this, Christ is definitely in charge; there was no doubt about His lordship. But His style of lordship turns authority right side up for the first time in history. He becomes a servant-lord. Inherent to servanthood are a submissive attitude and spirit that hold up other people. I believe this to be the model for the Christian husband.

David and Nancy Low are one of the exciting young couples we have met since coming to Washington. He is a financial lawyer, and she is a top-flight public relations administrator. Only recently have they come to Washington, and the reason for their coming is a good illustration of a servant-head of a home.

After working in another state for a well-known and respected political leader, Nancy was offered a very high position in a federal government agency. This opportunity was made even more exciting by the fact that it had never before been offered to a woman. David felt the offer was a high honor and urged Nancy to accept. He was confident he could find a job in his field in Washington. So, submitting to Nancy's career potential, they pulled up·stakes and settled here.

Some men would be threatened by this type of situation. If a man wanted to prove that he didn't need other people, if he were an emotional do-it-yourselfer, then he might resist the emergence of his wife's career, especially if it was an outstanding one. But David is a strong man, eager and able to become a servant to Nancy's development. That is healthy "headship" and management.

Modern corporate management has taken a page right out of our book and handed it back to the Christian home. Douglas McGregor, in *The Human Side of Enterprise*, speaks of x-style and y-style managers. The x-style managers are the authoritarian decision makers who hand down their executive memos each morning and watch their "good" vice-presidents doing exactly what they are told. These managers have greatly restricted their enterprises to the limits of their own creative abilities and mistakes. They leave little room for the growth and development of others unless that growth happens to coincide with the interests of the "big shot." So much potential goes to waste in corporations under this sort of management that it is no wonder morale is often low. People don't like to be kept down or left out of decision-making that affects them.

The y-style managers, on the other hand, guarantee a process in which others can devlop under their leadership. They watch for others' strengths with which to meet the various corporate needs, provide the resources for their development, and give over responsibility while keeping communication close. No wonder morale is high in corporations where persons are encouraged to grow to their full potential!

When Christ delegated authority to His disciples, He focused on their personal liberation and development— not subjugation.

Why not apply this concept to the home? I believe the husband *is* the head of the house. The question for me is not, "Who's in charge here?" but rather, "What sort of leadership is being exercised?" There are x-style and y-style husbands. Colleen and I are deeply concerned about the heavy emphasis on x-style husbands in many manuals on the Christian home. Instead of calling forth the abilities of others, these husbands act like little generals ordering their troops around and demanding submission on all points. Or they gallantly try to be "the fearless leader" in *all* aspects of their homes, even in areas where they are not gifted. In living out the x-style they deny the servant role and fail to resource others to their development in the home. Everybody feels their awkwardness and embarrassment. Heavy burdens, indeed!

Marriage works best when the husband uses his authority to create an atmosphere in which the potentials of each member of the family are identified, stimulated, and nurtured. Most of us learn best from example, or an almost unconscious observation of others we admire. In our generation we need to build strong new models that will demonstrate how beautiful *mutual* submission and fulfillment can be.

I love flying! And I have had both styles of instructors. The x-style often use four-letter words to impress their students with their toughness, and they usually flaunt a superior attitude. I remember one who got into the plane and said nothing. There I was, waiting for some indication of what the lesson of the day would be, and—nothing but silence. Finally the instructor grumped, "Well, you want to fly or not? What are you waiting for?" Then, without giving me a moment to reply, he blurted out. "Ever heard of ground effect?"

I hesitated for a moment and was just about to explain what I knew when he sarcastically retorted, "I didn't think so!"

Once aloft we were doing some stalls, and I failed to give sufficient rudder to compensate for the torque of the engine. Suddenly, he stomped on the right rudder pedal and almost shouted, "Don't you ever use any rudder?" Needless to say, it wasn't much of a lesson, and I noticed he wasn't around the next time I went out.

The y-type instructor was encouraging. After explaining the situation before we got into the plane, he asked if there were any questions about the previous gound-school lesson. Once we were in the air, he affirmed whatever maneuvers he could, correcting only what was necessary. He left me with a feeling that I wanted to be the best pilot I could be. How I worked for that man! He created an attitude about flying that not only enabled me to manipulate an airplane but gave me a basis for determining when I should fly and when I shouldn't. There was a quiet authority in his teaching. He left no doubt about who was PIC (pilot in command), yet increasingly he encouraged me to make my own decisions and develop professional procedures. He was a servant to my emergence as a pilot.

When Christ created each member of a family with creative potential, he didn't expect that potential to be buried under a blanket of restrictions or hidden in a closet of frustrations. He did not mean for a wife, or children, to submit to a false authority rooted in an unhealthy or insecure male ego. No entity is better suited than the family to bring about human development, and that is the responsibility of the head of the home.

Who's in charge here? *Jesus Christ.* And in reverence to Him, a husband—a servant-head to his wife and children, sacrificing for their development—and a wife, exercising the authority that accompanies her gifts, ministering to her husband, her children, and her world. As these two grow together, under Christ, they become the exciting, mature persons the world is "standing on tiptoe . . . to see coming into their own" (Rom. 8:19, PH).

4 Communication:

Affirming the Joy and Working through the Tough Times

by Coke

It was a beautiful spring evening in the hills of Bel Air, California. The scent of night-blooming jasmine came through the open windows on the wings of a gentle breeze, and it seemed that all was well in the world.

Getting ready for the evening service of the new church Louie had been called to start, I was standing in front of the big mirror in our bathroom, brushing my hair. I remember hearing the front door open and close as people began to congregate in our living room for the service.

Our life since arriving in Bel Air had been a fast track—a constant round of calls, meetings, and people. It wasn't that Louie and I were never together—just so rarely *alone*. It had been weeks since we had had an evening for ourselves. I was tired. We had four babies under five years of age, and a home that doubled as a church office, sanctuary, and fellowship hall. But more than being tired, I was in some strange way lonely. I loved our work. I was as excited about it as Louie was. Our people were marvelous. But something was wrong, and I was just beginning to wrestle with whatever it was.

At that point, Louie, who had been out visiting new members, entered the room catch his breath and freshen up before facing the growing crowd of people filling our living room.

There he was, standing beside me, washing his hands. He was so excited about the calls he had just made, thrilled with what God was doing in the lives of people in our fellowship, and eagerly planning the next project—and the next, and the next.

Now as a good wife, I, of course, shared his enthusiasm, right? Wrong! The more he talked and the more excited he became, the more I struggled with my churning insides. My feelings rose higher and higher, that lump in my throat got bigger, and finally the tears spilled over the top, and I let him have it. Poor Louie! All those people in the living room waiting to be inspired, and his wife dissolves in tears in the bathroom. But as I stomped my foot and my trembling voice wrapped words around my feelings, he listened. I'll always be grateful to him for that.

I'm not sure exactly what I said, but between sniffs and sobs I was somehow able to tell Louie about the need I was just beginning to sense within myself. I told him how hungry I was to be with him, to have time to talk and dream, alone. I shared my strong feeling that there had to be a change in our relentless schedule, a change that would give us time to communicate and build our relationship. Even as I spoke, the conviction that there was no way we could continue nurturing others if we did not make a commitment to nurturing our own relationship, became crystal clear.

Well, there obviously wasn't time for Louie to hear me out completely just then, but later, after the meeting was over and the door had closed for the last time, he did. We sat and talked for a very long time, saying things we both wanted and needed to hear, things we had been almost too busy to think, much less say to one another!

Although he was hurting, I remember Louie thanked me for being honest about my feelings. That meant something special to me. He also agreed that indeed we did need to slow down in order to make time to nurture our own relationship.

And then he did a simple, practical and, to me, very beautiful thing. He took his little date book from his pocket and looked until he found a free night. It happened to be Thursday of the following week, and he said, "That's our night." And so it was the next week that we had an evening all to ourselves. It was wonderful. And out of that night came a decision to put aside time every week for the same purpose, and so it has been in all the years since. Thursday night is our night.

Now I'm sure many couples are able to *find* time for each other in an easy, unscheduled way, and that's ideal. But that didn't work for us. With our kind of life we found we had to *make* time, literally grabbing hold of our schedules and writing it into our date books. And that was one of the most important decisions we ever made. It gave our relationship a clear sense of priority and the time we need to say, "This is where I am, where are you?" For any marriage or any relationship of depth will only be as good as its communication. And communication takes time!

It also takes *energy*, for communication is not just talking *to* or *at* someone. It is sharing our *real* feelings. It is sharing what we think, value, fear, hate, dream, and believe. It is also expressing affirmation for our spouse. God help the couple whose communication dwells only on the negative. In marriage we need to be radically affirming, making *certain* our husband or wife knows we delight in them. And when we feel a sudden, unexpected rush of affection and warmth, *telling* them, at the risk of sounding corny, that they bring joy to every fiber of our being.

Communication is part of being an authentic person,

saying what we feel and feeling what we say. We communicate in many different ways at the same time, so that even the sharing of a few words can send a very complicated message. In fact, whether we speak or not, in an intimate relationship we are constantly sending and receiving messages. We can speak volumes with a look, a tone of voice, or a touch on the shoulder as we pass our partner's chair at the family table. In fact, a large part of communication is being sensitively aware of our mate and this sensitivity is expressed in simple ways: our asking, listening, noticing, touching, remembering. As we open ourselves up to one another we grow in our authenticity as people, for in a way I must be able to transparently share who I am with my husband in order to *know* who *I* am.

The cry for communication is loud and persistent! A recent national survey indicated that lack of communication was the highest cause of marital failure. Again and again, the chief complaint was, "We just can't talk to each other." I know it is true among women. I hear this hunger expressed more than any other: "If only my husband would talk to me!" "We just *don't* communicate." Or, "He's so busy making money! I don't want his money; I want *him!*"

Women are hungry for their men—hungry to know and be known. But it doesn't go only one way. Men too have this basic desire, and how healthy it is that our society is finally granting its permission for men to express their needs openly. The drive we feel to know and be known is not linked to our sex but to our basic humanity. We want it so much because God created us to have it.

Many couples begin marriage convinced that nothing will take away the closeness they feel. Somehow they miss the truth that love and communication go hand in hand and must be worked at or else, like unused muscles, they will atrophy from disuse.

I'm thinking of a couple we know. They were ecstatic when they first got married, and they remained happy for a few years. He enjoyed his work; she enjoyed being at home with the children. They looked forward to seeing each other at the end of each day. On weekends they had fun together. Then, very gradually, it all began to change. At night when he came home they found themselves saying the same things to each other. He was preoccupied, and she felt she was intruding when she asked him questions about his job. Yet she wanted so much to talk to him! All day, every day, she was with the children. They lived in a very small town where, in her opinion, nothing exciting seemed to happen, and she longed for him to tell her what went on in the city where people were busy doing interesting things. She tried to make conversations of her own, but what could she talk about except the people she saw at the supermarket or how her quarters got stuck in the dry cleaning machine. Finally one evening he snapped, "I don't want to hear about that stuff! It's boring!" He might just as well have said *she* was boring, and maybe she was. At least in her mind, it was so. His work and the people he met were so fascinating. How could she keep up with them?

As time passed, her husband learned to block out what he didn't like or want to hear, and their marriage hit a dangerous low. When communication is only on a superficial, trivial level, never coming to grips with true feelings, a great deal of what is said is "tuned out."

That happens to a lot of marriages. According to a study done by a group of psychiatrists, the average man and wife communicate with each other for 28 minutes a week. They may talk a lot more than that, and they may transmit messages in ways other than verbal, but obviously they aren't getting through to each other. And if they aren't getting through, they aren't communicating!

That reminds me of something Paul Tournier wrote:

"Listen to all the conversations of our world, between nations as well as those between couples. They are for the most part dialogues of the deaf" (*Marriage Difficulties*, SCM Press, p. 8).

So that we do not conduct dialogues of the deaf, we need to work on our communication in marriage. As and as we do there is much we can learn from God's Word, which is so direct, so transparent, and yet always so full of care for people. When God led James to write, "Let your yes be yes and your no be no" (James 5:12), He was guiding us toward simplicity, clarity, and directness. Communication is an art that *can* be learned. We can learn to listen and not tune out our partner. We can learn to say it straight ourselves, and then not misinterpret what our spouse is saying. Some people call it *truthing it*—that is, *speaking the truth in love* (Eph. 4:15). Truthing it is a term used in David Augsburger's *The Love-Fight*.

Lately, in my own life, as I've been working on truthing, I have been trying to learn to *speak* more accurately. It's too easy for me to say "others feel," when what I really mean is "I feel." I also have noticed that when Louie and I are talking, I am inclined to want to speak for him: "I feel you feel that I feel." In my journey toward transparency, I would like to let others speak for themselves, as I accept the responsibility I have to speak for myself. This is part of truthing it—and truthing it is good for communication.

Listening

But truthing it is not just speaking the truth. It is also *hearing* the truth, being open to the truth about ourselves. And this is another area on which I need to work. When I listen, I want to hear truly. I don't want to block out what my husband or others might be trying to say to me simply because they are saying things I might not like to hear.

When I listen to my husband, I want to hear what *he* feels, not what I feel. Not hearing feelings can be a stumbling block in the way of being a true listener. I remember a time in our marriage when Louie was feeling particularly inadequate about his work. He really doubted his teaching and preaching ability, and it was a painful period for him. He tried to tell me what he was feeling, but I thought he was so gifted, so strong in these areas, that I couldn't hear him when he said he was hurting. My repeated affirmations—"I'd rather listen to you preach than *anyone*," and "I learn so much when you teach"—fell on deaf ears. What I felt *about* him was getting in the way of my hearing *him*. Finally he convinced me. To my amazement I saw that at that time and place he really *did* feel inadequate. It was only then that I was able to hear him, to feel *with* him, and to walk with him during a dark time.

Another very real part of communciation is conflict, learning how to talk and work through the tough times. In his wonderful little book, *Why Am I Afraid to Tell You Who I Am?* John Powell says:

> All deep and authentic friendships, and especially the union of those who are married, must be based on absolute openness and honesty. At times, gut-level communication will be most difficult, but it is at these precise times that it is necessary (Argus Communications, pp. 61-2).

I agree. Gut-level communication is difficult and risky, but if a couple has enough faith in the strength of their relationship, they can take the risk. The greater risk is to avoid it out of fear of conflict.

If we are still battling the fear of being rejected, we will see conflict as a crushing threat. "If we clash, you may reject me." Most marriages have to grow in their ability to handle conflicts in a natural way. *Ours* certain-

ly did! In our early years together we were great at
sharing the positive, joyous parts of our relationship.
However, coming to grips with the painful areas of conflict that quite naturally arose from time to time was
another matter. I think we unconsciously saw conflict as
some sinister threat to our relationship and so avoided it
whenever possible. But as the years passed, fortunately—for our marriage—our perception of conflict began
to change. Our life together was teaching us that when
two people are in intimate emotional, physical, and
spiritual contact, a kind of ambivalence and conflict is
inevitable. Moreover, as we *began* to risk sharing at the
point of our conflict, we discovered that it was not the
threatening enemy after all. It was instead a friend helping us understand one another on a deeper level. We
saw that in closing off tender areas we may have avoided momentary pain, but we had also limited our depth
and closeness. We also saw that God was using conflict
as a catalyst to help us see and accept as healthy the
adjustments we had to make if our marriage were going
to continue to grow into the kind of relationship God
intended it to be.

And so we made a decision to "go for it," to risk
talking honestly about our conflicts, as well as our joys,
an integral part of our commitment to one another. We
took as our guide for working through the tough times,
Ephesians 4:26, "Be angry but do not sin; do not let the
sun go down on your anger." This means we look for
the first possible *appropriate* time to work out a difference. (I try not to open up a heavy discussion on Satur-
day night when Louie is getting all geared up for three
sermons on Sunday morning!)

Over the years, this decision has cost literally hun-
dreds of hours of energy-draining communication, as
well as some pure and simple emotional discomfort and
pain. However, the time and tears have been a small
price indeed for the genuine closeness they have

brought, and the opportunity they continue to provide to deepen our relationship.

But many couples are light-years ahead of where we were when we were newly married, and I'm glad. Having been warned about, or just innately understanding the inevitability of ambivalence and conflict in any close relationship, they begin marriage with the understanding that honesty will not only be allowed, but will be encouraged.

In his sensitive book *I Loved a Girl*, Walter Trobisch writes:

> Before he was married, one of my friends wrote to his fiancee about what he expected from his future wife.
>
> "She must challenge me to the highest degree by completely honest criticism of me.
>
> "When she is disappointed in me, she must not withdraw her confidence.
>
> "She must never pretend, but must tell me honestly when I have hurt her."
>
> Do you understand? What he wanted was not a servant girl, but an equal partner who stands beside him before God. Only with such a partner can you become "one flesh" in the real depths of its meaning—a new living being. Partnership includes the right to criticize (Harper & Row, p. 48).

Along the same line, I like what Bruce Larson says on "Being Real People":

> Jesus brought reality to every encounter, and that is another important dimension of love. A genuine lover is not plastic or falsely pious or always in control. Real people can get angry from time to time. Jesus got angry when He saw what was hap-

pening in God's house, and He made a whip and drove the money changers out of the temple. My friend Charlie Shedd, Presbyterian clergyman and noted author and lecturer, tells a story I love. One morning he came down to breakfast after having had a terrible fight with his wife, Martha, the night before. For the first time in their married life, Martha was not there making breakfast. She had left the house. He found a note propped up by the sugar bowl. It said, "Dear Charlie: I hate you. (Signed) Love, Martha." That's what love is all about. Love is being able to say, "I love you." But it is also being able to say on occasion, "I hate you." If we can't express anger, we probably can't love (*There's a Lot More to Being Healthy than Not Being Sick*, Word Publishing, p. 115).

You see, conflict *isn't* bad; it is a natural part of any deep, caring relationship. It is precisely because marriage *is* so close and intimate that it also has such a high susceptibility to conflict. But it can even be fun when it's dealt with as quickly as possible, openly and with love and respect. Of course it isn't *always* fun. Conflict can be very painful for me, but that does not give me reason to fear it or run from it. How we handle our hassles, and work through our differences and conflicts, tells much about the kind of people we are. It also tells us something about our philosophy and the goals for our marriage. If peace is our objective, we may not dare to risk conflict. But if a creative *growing* relationship is our desire, we must.

Steps of Communication
In working through problems and conflicts there are some steps, or dynamics, of communication that can be helpful. Because these steps have worked for people we know, and for us, I would like to share them in the hope

that they will be useful to someone else in a time of need. I like them, not because they are foolproof (they're not), but because they offer couples the opportunity to minister to one another in the process.

First, if one partner is angry and troubled by a problem or situation, the other partner has to resist counterattacking and just hold his/her tongue for a while. That does not mean he/she becomes a doormat or a target for abuse. Perhaps for a short time he/she has to be dumped on, but the important thing is that he/she gives the other person a chance to unburden.

The listener is the minister to the other. Sometimes he/she may have to try to extract whatever it is that has built up inside the other. Perhaps a husband needs to talk out a painful problem he has with his boss. Perhaps a wife is troubled by an interfering mother, or she may be having problems with *her* boss. Maybe something in *their* relationship is painful. Whatever it is, it has to come out, and it never will if both partners are wounding each other with their angry barbs.

When the listening partner feels that the other has finally gotten it all out, that's the time to go back over the same ground, asking, "Is this how you feel? Am I getting it right?" This does not mean agreeing with the other person; it's simply trying to determine where the other person is. Perhaps the listener will have to be corrected a few times, but finally they should both be able to say, "Yes, I understand."

Second, now that the dark river has begun to dissipate, the clear stream of insight can begin to flow. The ministering one continues to listen, giving the other partner the freedom to explore the causes and sources of their anger. It's important for the listener to refrain from making any suggestions of their own. This is where I have to watch myself. I'm a hopeless "fixer" and have to hold my tongue to keep from telling Louie just what he should do about a problem even before he is finished telling me the whole story. He has to remind me often by saying, "Cokie, please, I just want you to *listen!*" Let the other person identify his/her own problem, even if it is as difficult for you as it is for me.

Third, once a partner knows what is bothering them, they can begin to consider alternative solutions. Again, the listening partner shouldn't try to impose answers on the other, although they can help to explore the solutions open to the other person. If a boss is domineering, or if a mother is the kind who tries to tell a wife how to bring up her children, what can the other person do about it? And what might the outcome be? Perhaps these same alternatives occurred to the troubled person earlier, but because they couldn't articulate them, they seemed too risky. Now that they are able to talk about them with an understanding listener, they may see their problem in a new light. Perhaps a husband will decide that he needs to do something drastic such as change his job. Or he may decide that he can handle his anger at work without taking it out on his wife at home. Perhaps a wife will decide that there is a way she can encounter her mother without destroying their relationship. If the problem is in their own marriage relationship, the area will be more tender and vulnerable for both of them, for such is the way of love. And at this point perhaps one partner may be able to say to the other, "Honey, just the fact that I'm talking this out with you makes me feel better."

Fourth, any decision made immediately after an outburst of anger should be reconsidered later. Sometimes, in the wake of an emotional explosion, a person is so eager to compromise that they may reget their decision later. So, after a day or two, the listening partner should talk over the decision with the other, asking, "Is this what you meant? Is this what we agreed to do?" If the other person has second thoughts, the decision should be altered.

Fifth, when each partner knows how the troubled one is going to deal with the source of their anger, is the problem solved? Will there never be another outburst over this same issue? Not on your life! Here is where the ministering partner must be *patient* and *prayerful*—two of the best ways to support the one he/she loves.

Usually the problem is caused by a deep habit pattern. If we human beings were able to change direction on a dime, our lives would be so different. But because many of our responses are conditioned over long periods of time, our old habits usually linger for a while after we begin asking God to break us free of them. As Corrie ten Boom says, "After you stop ringing a bell, there may be a few *dings* left." No matter how vehemently one partner proclaims that he or she is going to change, there's the chance that that partner will get into the same rut again—possibly again and again.

What does the ministering partner do when that happens? Do we say, "You dope! You blew it!" Not if we have faith in the other person's potential. Instead of making the other partner feel like a failure because they goofed, the ministering partner says, "I'm hanging in there with you. I know it's tough, but I'm praying with you, and with God's help, I know you can do it." And when the day comes that the old response gives way to a new one, no one is more grateful than the ministering partner.

This process of communication is one more way of submitting to the need of one partner to be heard and understood. In the last thirty years, Louie has submitted to me many times, and I to him, in this way. We don't take turns or keep score. This happens when it needs to happen. It takes time, emotional energy, and patience on the part of the listener, but the reward of SHALOM (the real peace that comes after struggle) is worth it all; so we are grateful for the process. As one couple who have grown in their ability to share deeply put it: "Now we can talk as two human beings instead of paper dolls labeled 'wife' and 'husband.'"

But it *is* just a process—helpful in some situations, but certainly not in all. There are those times in every relationship when words have no more meaning unless there is a genuine expression of repentance. It is so deeply healing to be able to confess failure, weakness, stubbornness, and insensitivity—whatever comes between—even if you feel your partner has as much to confess as you. When we can come to see that our husband's or wife's response in any situation is *their* responsibility, and our response is ours, we have arrived at a mature and healthy place. We are also relieved of the role and burden of being judge in another's life; a role only God should assume.

The Book of Proverbs tells us that love covers all transgressions and even forgets mistakes (Proverbs 10:12; 17:9). In our marriages, *every* one of them, there will be those times when only this kind of love will get us through. It is a love so radical only God could be its source, and it is available to everyone of us willing to receive. It is *this* love that enables us to forgive our spouse *anything*. And this same love enables *us* to take charge of our own response so we can communicate sincerely the most powerful healing message a wife or husband can ever give the other:

"I'm sorry -
Please forgive me"
"I love you."

These simple words are the *sine qua non* of communication for the "very married." Or so they have become for us.

Communication is work. It is costly, but it is one of the best investments any of us who are married can ever make.

5 Gifts:
Growth through Love's Support

by Louie

by Louie

Three o'clock in the afternoon is not my best time for counseling. I suppose the problem is that my body considers it well past the time for a midday nap and refuses to stand at the duty station. Sometimes it can be an awful experience just trying to keep my eyes open.

On one particular afternoon I looked with groggy eyes at my date book to check on my next appointment. I perked up immediately when I saw the names of a young man and woman I had recently married. They were a delightful couple who always left me with a deposit of joy. Their premarital counseling had been a happy experience for me. They were always full of questions, and they explored new ideas and concepts like a couple of avid mountain climbers attacking a new peak. One of the agreements we made was that they would come back from time to time to talk over their growth, their ideas, and any problems they wanted to share.

The next hour was no disappointment. They were dressed casually and their eyes danced with joy. They were alive with a new idea! I wondered what it would be this time.

"Something you said in our premarital sessions meant

55

a lot to us, and we have been trying to work it out. We think we have. Would you like to hear it?"

"Don't keep me in suspense," I said as I motioned them toward a couch.

"You know how much Christ has meant to us and to the kids we work with in Young Life. Well, we have been discovering something about gifts of the Holy Spirit—in marriage, that is."

For the moment my mind turned to the charismatic emphasis that is alive in Washington—gifts of the Spirit characterized by speaking in tongues, prophesying, and healing. But Fred and Marcia meant something else.

"We are discovering gifts in our marriage," Marcia explained. "Not roles determined strictly by sex, but by the abilities the Holy Spirit has given each of us."

"Oh, true enough," Fred chimed in, "I'm the head of the house. We believe the man is the head of the house, just as Paul said. And, yes, Marcia is going to have the babies. But in our counseling we liked the idea of my being a 'servant-head.' Like Christ, I want my authority to be used to help Marcia realize her gifts of the Spirit. And that goes for the little one, too," he said with a cat-ate-the-mouse look toward his wife.

"Is this some kind of announcement?" I questioned.

"I guess so," she confirmed, "and we're thrilled about it. What we are saying includes the baby, too. Can we share this new insight with you?"

"Go ahead."

"Fred says he doesn't want me to give up my career at the medical lab. We've decided on two children, and of course I'm going to be a full-time mother while they are young. But when they are in nursery school, I'll go back to work part-time. Fred and I agree that the children need both a mother and a father, so he is going to take time to be with them some part of each day. That will mean some planning, such as where we are going to live. We don't want Fred to live so far from his work that commuting eats up two hours a day. It will also mean limiting our nighttime activities. We'll have to cut down on some of our church work, so the kids won't be church orphans."

"I feel the children need to experience tenderness and care from their dad as well as their mother," Fred said. "So it will be my job to bathe the tykes and get them ready for bed, which will also give Marcia relief at the end of the day. But on top of that, each of these little ones will have some potential for development, and I want to share in the fun of finding out what that is. Then I want to help them develop it. Maybe that's selfish of me, but that's the way I feel."

"I think it's great!" I responded.

Perhaps Fred and Marcia are learning early in their marriage what it had taken Colleen and me some years to discover; when a person comes to Christ, one of the most exciting things that happens is that he or she receives a gift, or gifts, of the Spirit. These gifts are meant to be used for the common good in the body of Christ, and the great joy of having them comes from knowing that one has a place in the family of God. And who does not need to be needed?

In the past, roles were more clearly defined, and very often determined, not by gifts, but by sex and society.

In a way, these predetermined roles kept husbands and wives in their own arenas, so they didn't get in each other's way.

Today, there is much more overlap, even switching of roles as gifts are discovered that just don't fit the old pattern for doing things. This overlap can cause conflict, of course. On the other hand, it can be a great opportunity for deep companionship and joy.

Gifts of the Spirit
A gift of the Spirit is an ability to fulfill a need in the body of Christ. Whatever function is needed, the Spirit

designs a gift and gives it to an available channel. When we say it is given for the common good, we mean it is to be used for another's benefit.

God is a practical God who wants to see provision made for His children. He wants His body to function for the sake of the lost world He still loves very much. When all the parts are working properly, the body grows vigorously and a deep interdependence emerges so that when one member suffers, the whole body suffers together. If one rejoices, all the parts rejoice together.

Obviously the gifts of the Spirit are given without reference to sex. Just as there was no difference in the dominion given to male and female in the Creation, so there is no sex basis for receiving the gifts of the Spirit. The Prophet Joel, foretelling the coming of the Holy Spirit, predicted: "And it shall come to pass afterward, that I will pour out My spirit on all flesh; your *sons* and your *daughters* shall prophesy, your old men shall dream dreams, and your young men shall see visions" (Joel 2:28, author's italics).

Luke also speaks of the four daughters of Philip the Evangelist exercising their gift of prophecy. "And the next day we . . . entered into the house of Philip the evangelist, which was one of the seven; and abode with him. And the same man had four daughters, virgins, which did prophesy" (Acts 21:8-9, KJV). Paul described prophesying as the highest of the gifts (1 Cor. 14). Evidently the gifts of the Spirit were for both male and female alike, with no distinction based on sex.

In the presently renewed interest in the gifts of the Spirit, some have held rather strict interpretation as to the number and identity of the gifts; some say there are five gifts, some eight, and others claim twelve. Looking at the varying lists Paul mentions, I do not believe he was enumerating only so many gifts and no more. The table below illustrates my point.

Lists of the Gifts of the Spirit

Romans 12:6-8	1 Corinthians 12:7-10	1 Corinthians 12:28	Ephesians 4:11-12
Prophecy	Wisdom	Apostles	Apostles
Service	Knowledge	Prophets	Prophets
Teaching	Faith	Teachers	Evangelists
Exhorting	Healing	Workers	Pastors
Contributing	Miracles	of miracles	Teachers
Giving Aid	Prophecy	Healers	
Ruling	Discernment	Helpers	
	Tongues	Administrators	
	Interpretation	Speakers in	
	of tongues	Tongues	

I believe the apostle had in mind a broader meaning of the gifts based on the varying *needs* of the early church. God is wonderfully practical: If His church has a need, He gives some saint the ability to fill that need. If the needs change, so does his provision of the gifts. There must be a great deal of latitude in the broad categories designated "service," "helps," "giving aid," and "administration." The recipients of the last gift must certainly have different roles today than in the early church. With our complex church structures, intricate budgets, tax complexities, personnel requirements, mechanical maintenance, and numerous details, I am sure the Lord has given some persons the ability to administer them in a complex age. I believe it because I work with such persons. If there is a need, God's Spirit creates a gift to meet that need. It is as broad and simple as that.

So it is with the home! God provides gifts of His Spirit within the home irrespective of sex—except, of course, for the obvious specialized ability of women to bear children, and of men to sire them, and perhaps a few others. Some women have the gift of financial management, and some husbands that of cooking. Some women have the gift of spiritual teaching, and some husbands the gift of sensitive discernment. The thrill of a marriage is the continuous discovery of one another's gifts, and as the seasons of marriage change, so do some of the gifts.

Seasons may change the roles and gifts; circumstances may do the same within a marriage.

We know a couple whose roles have been changed by a serious illness that left the husband semiparalyzed and unable to continue in his profession. His wife has gone to work and discovered gifts she never dreamed she had—resulting in a highly creative and successful career. The husband laughs about being a "house-husband," but seems to thoroughly enjoy his new role. He has become a gourmet cook and runs their home like a pro. There is a sweetness in their relationship that comes, I believe, from their mutual submission to changing times and gifts.

Finance is an area many people think belongs in the husband's basket. But must it always be so? Suppose the husband doesn't have such a gift. In the home where I grew up, it was my mother who managed the finances. Even though Dad made the final decisions, it was Mother who supplied the data and the counsel by which those decisions were made. I think God knew that He would use Dad in a way that would leave little time for anything other than his ministry, so He equipped Mother to manage the household finances.

Granted that God creates and provides the gifts; how, then, are we to discover them?

Gift Discovery
There probably will be little gift discovery unless the Christian is actively engaged in the body of Christ. We are not very good at discovering who we really are and what we do best, if we live only unto ourselves. In our homes, primarily, and then in the church and society, we discover who we are as we interrelate with others. Prayer may certainly be one of the methods, but seldom

is prayer effective without some input from our brothers and sisters, the body of Christ.

For instance, one of the ways we discover who we are is through the *honesty* of others. The best illustration I can share is from my own experience.

Administrative detail is *not* one of my gifts. Even on our wedding day I was working up to the last minute, barely getting ready in time for the ceremony. But Coke had completed her work two days early and spent the day relaxing and reading. At times I let things go longer than I should. Oh, yes, I can plead the pressure of demands and all that sort of thing, but while I am making excuses, my wife gets things done quietly, quickly, and early.

At times Coke will exercise her honesty and bring to my attention something only I can do that really needs to be done. I know I should be grateful, yet I'll have to admit that I resist her honesty—less now than previously, I must hurry to add. Her reminder touches my guilt buttons, and my lights of defensive reaction go on. But recently, as I have been submitting to her honesty, we have discovered one of her gifts in our marriage. It's what we might call "discerning administration," or an ability to sense what is needed and important, and then doing something about the matter without any last minute hassles. This gift brings a sense of order to the body, whether in the church or in the home.

On the other side of the coin, although Coke is very adventuresome in life and philosophy, she does not like to take risks when it comes to physical safety. She wanted to keep that motherly protective ring around our children longer than I thought wise. One summer many years ago the children were striking out across a little lake—distance of about 400 yards—paddling plastic air mattresses like paddle boards. As Coke stood on the dock, calling them back with desperate "mommy noises," the kids turned around and called back that they were OK. Though tiny, they were good swimmers and knew how to rest on their backs in the water. I was quite sure they would come to one another's aid should anything happen to one of the rafts. Besides, the motorboat was close at hand and ready to go. I had to pull rank on Coke and exercise my gift, which was turning the children loose to their adventuresome exploits. At times I had to encounter her about her overprotectiveness, and though she wasn't jumping up and down she did is gracious enough to say that out of my honesty and her discovery of my gift, she has been able to grow in that area.

Sensitive communication is a second way in which we discover our gifts. It happened to a pastor and his wife whose three active children had kept them busy and on their toes for years. Then the time came when the children left home, and the pastor's life settled down to the dull roar of administering one of the country's most creative churches. But something cruical had gone out of the home for the wife. Restlessness began to stalk her peace; an edge of sharpness replaced her patient reserved behavior. Because her husband was a sensitive and caring person, these changes did not escape his notice, and soon he was drawing his wife out in conversation. At first she felt pangs of guilt because she was dissatisfied with the usual role of a minister's wife. But her husband kept drawing out her feelings, saying they were more important than prescribed roles. "I'm married to you, not to the church," he said. As the wife allowed her feelings to flow, she and her husband began to realize that she was interested in counseling. Her desire to be involved in a ministry of therapy was so strong that she felt she wanted to work at a professional level. That meant a great deal of training, but with her husband's encouragement, she became a schoolgirl again in her mid-forties. She sailed through her B.A. degree, light-hearted as a lark. Her M.A. was captured with honors, and she trudged on toward her doctorate. It took years, but she did it. At times the stress took its toll upon their relationship, but they always talked things out, made the adjustments, and forged ahead. Now the wife has opened an office and has a very effective ministry of her own as she conducts her own therapeutic practice. And it all began with her husband's encouraging her to talk out what she felt—exercising her gift of sensitive communication.

Helping another person to get out what he or she is feeling *is* a gift. It's like "pulling the web out of the spider," which is a phrase I have to explain with a story.

As a boy I loved football; it was in my genes—the ones I got from Dad. Whenever we could, he and I went down to the Pitt Stadium to watch Pitt or Carnegie Tech play. One morning I had walked the two miles from our house to the church to meet my father, who had been counseling. A young man was just leaving as I knocked on the study door. For a moment we three stood on the steps leading out of my father's study, its gothic oak vault rising high overhead and its leaded windows letting in the soft light of a cool November day. A spider decided to make its appearance in our midst, hanging from a web right before our faces. The young man reached up, took the web and said, "Watch." Down, down, down went the spider until he had almost reached the floor, vainly struggling to gather in his web faster than it was being extricated from him. The young man took my hand and said, "Here, you try it." I shook the web, but too gently. The spider was gaining on me! Almost frantically I increased the sharpness of my shaking. Suddenly the web broke. Without a moment's delay, my friend picked up the web and got things going again. Then he took my hand and gave me the right rhythm and intensity. Out came the web, longer and longer.

Getting a person to talk about his feelings is like

shaking the web out of a spider. Too gently and he gets it all back inside. Too brusquely and the web of communication breaks. There is that gentle but persistent touch that helps one to get out what the other person is feeling. And as the other talks, an interest may begin to emerge. Like the web of a spider, a latent desire may appear before your very eyes. I like what John Powell says when he describes genuine love as that when two people "respect otherness in each other. Each person values and tries to promote the inner vision and mysterious destiny of the other" (*The Secret of Staying in Love*, Argus Communication, pp. 64-66).

A third way of discovering others' gifts is to *mirror another person's strengths*, to reflect to the other affirmatively what we feel his or her gift to be.

A couple Colleen and I came to know very well in seminary was a good example of the mirroring of affirmation. The husband had been very successful in his business for over eleven years, but a kind of restlessness pervaded all he did. His work didn't have the zing it once had.

The wife began to watch for her husband's high points, those moments of joy that gave him the greatest fulfillment. They turned out to be people-moments—occasions when, through his sensitivity, he was able to give insight to one of his colleagues. With a deft and smooth firmness he would bring warring parties together and inspire them to settle disputes. When it came to sharing his faith, he had a warm, down-to-earth reasonableness about him that was regularly bringing people to Christ. As his wife began to mirror back his high points, helping him to compare them with the low points of his business life, a mound of data began to grow. One day he said, "You know what, honey? I just might go into the ministry. What would you think of that? Scare ya?"

His wife had been raised in a Swedish pastor's family.

She knew the pressures and struggles, the leannesses and the tough times; but she also knew if this was of God there would be a deep satisfaction for her husband. "No," she said, "it doesn't scare me a bit! You'd make a great minister. Darling, I'm with you 100 percent, and I'm ready to start tomorrow!"

He decided to take a couple of days off to pray about it. He drove to his favorite retreat, a place where the fish played exciting games with lures before they struck. The second afternoon, after a good catch, a time of prayer, and a leisurely nap in the woods, he "woke up in the ministry." He is one of the most relaxed, effective pastors I've ever known.

In our own family I can see the children going to Coke for their heart-sharing; but they come to me for counsel on their religion or history papers. They are helping us to identify our gifts by mirroring responses to our strengths.

One more factor in the discovery of gifts is the willingness to *allow another to risk*. Discovery cannot take place unless there is an atmosphere of permission—a language that says, "Try it; see if it is for real."

A couple we knew many years ago did this, and it worked well for them. Betsy had been a nesting bird all through her marriage. Nothing gave her greater joy than providing for her husband and their children. But now that the two children were ready to "fly the nest," she was becoming progressively depressed. Finally she descended into a state that required hospitalization for a few days.

Betsy's husband was warmly sensitive and supportive during the recovery period as her anxiety rose and fell like waves. He helped her disengage from a number of her civic activities and affirmed her desire to work with her hands. Her sewing was full of creative and innovative ideas; cleverness of design marked everything she did. A mixture of practicality and striking art made her products go like hot cakes at bazaars. She thought of starting a gift shop, but her low self-image took care of that! She had almost no sense of self-worth. "Try it," her husband would say. "Don't bite the whole thing off at once, but work in someone else's shop for a while to see if you like it." So she got a part-time job, and he drove her to the shop three times a week. Bit by bit her assurance began to grow; she tried it and she liked it! Without her husband's encouragement, she probably would have stayed in her cave, peering fearfully out at a world where she saw others playing joyfully at the things she liked. But with one who loved her saying, "Try it," she found the strength and "took a cut at it." She discoverd a gift and a new business to boot—one that through the years has blessed her and others.

Gift Development

Once love aids in the process of discovery, the next phase of gift development gets underway. Love provides resources for the development of another's gift.

In a previous chapter we spoke of the type of leadership that is essential for gift development. In the home where the husband is exercising the y (or servant) style of leadership, he will not only permit but will stimulate the growth of others in his home. Because gifts have their own authority, he will allow other members of the family to *exercise the authority* that accompanies their gift.

Coke has the gift of "pacing," and when she uses it she does so with an authority I must take seriously. My natural tendency is to run the ship at full speed all the time. Needless to say, the whole crew gets worn out, and so does the skipper. And when the skipper gets worn out, he reacts in ways that can make shipboard life a hassle. It's about that time that the senior medical officer comes charging out of her stateroom, resolutely mounts the ladder to the bridge and says, "Captain, slow this vessel down! In fact, put into port for a few days!

We all need some R and R." And believe me, I have learned to follow the advice of the medical officer. She knows whereof she speaks!

Another way in which love resources development is by *providing time* for the other person to exercise his or her gift. A husband, or wife for that matter, can be so demanding of the other's time that any possibility of gift development is buried under a mountain of things to do. And buried deeply! In fact, this can become a means of keeping a mate from the development of a potential.

To give Coke an opportunity to cultivate her writing ability, the children and I had to decrease our demands on her time. She felt she needed quiet times in which to create—not little crumbs of minutes here and there but solid blocks of hours when an idea could grow without being scorched by the searing winds of constant demands. She thought Tuesdays and Thursdays were the best times. On Mondays she would get a good start on the week and clear up a lot of home and administrative details. Wednesdays she saved for church interests. On Thursdays I was at the church with the staff all day, which cut off any chance of our getting together. But her new routine meant no guests for dinner on Tuesday or Thursday nights, otherwise another gift of hers, that of hospitality, would demand spending half the day preparing for the guests. So, no surprises on Tuesdays or Thursdays! No phone calls at the last minute to ask, "How about a few extras for dinner tonight?" OK on other days, but Tuesdays and Thursdays were "no-nos."

Financial resources are often necessary for the development of another's gifts, and love makes the sacrifice to free them. Fen was a notably successful doctor. He and Joyce had four college-age children. Gradually Joyce felt a lifelong ambition catching fire again—she wanted to become a high-level administrative assistant. She knew she had the problem-solving abilities and the public relations "savvy" to do the job. But training would be needed. That meant money, and a fair amount at that, for tuition at a top-flight executive training institute!

"Any chance, Fen?" she asked timidly.

"Honey, no way," he retorted without hesitation. "We couldn't afford it. You know that!"

That was just the point: Joyce knew differently. She kept Fen's books. She saw as much as $17,000 go down the drain one month for repairs to his yacht, and there was the light, twin-engine aircraft he maintained for his own pleasure. Month after month Joyce made out checks totaling several thousand dollars to pay for Fen's "playing." He had plenty of chances to put the boat and the plane on lease-back arrangements, but he insisted that he "might want them at a moment's notice" and so held on to them like a little boy selfishly guarding his toys. Out of a $150,000-a-year practice, he could not break loose $5,000 to a wife who was doing at least a $20,000-a-year job of business and financial management for him, to say nothing of writing some of his medical speeches and papers.

On top of that, Fen dallied and reneged on so many promises to support the children in their advanced education that they failed to get into school and had to work to save enough money to go to college at all. Now, I'm for children working to help with their educational expenses, but the communication that came through loud and clear from Fen was, "After me, you come *third!*"

Today Fen has left his family and is still running around like a teenager trying to find himself. His wife has accomplished her goal and is carrying out a great ministry for God, but not without the pain of rejection still throbbing in her life. Fen was not about to provide resources for her as a person—much less work toward the development of her gift.

One of the greatest stimuli to development is good old *encouragement* or *affirmation*. In the marriage ceremony there is a question asked of the couple: "[So-and-so], will you have this [woman/man] to be your [wife/husband] and will you pledge your troth to [her/him] in all love and honor, in all duty and service, in all *faith* and tenderness?" The assenting parties are then to say, "I will."

In using the word *faith*, I mean not only fidelity in the sexual relationship but faith *in the person*. "I know you can make it" are the magic words that give many of us the courage to try and keep trying. And they may have to be said many times. For someone to throw up his hands and say, "Oh, there's no use! You'll never make it!" is one of the most rejecting, demotivating things that can happen to a person. True, some of us take that as an extra stimulus and try all the harder to prove ourselves. The only trouble is, we seldom quit trying to prove, and our whole life becomes a game of "I told you I could!" When I see someone putting others down in ruthless competition, I can't help but feel that there has been precious little faith-input logged into the computer of that persons's disposition.

The term *faith-input* reminds me of a pastor's family in Pittsburgh, Pennsylvania. They lived in the simplest circumstances, close by the car line where the pastor could take the streetcar to the church most days. The parents saw their two hardworking children through medical school and music conservatory by living frugally, borrowing, whenever necessary, sums that took them years to repay. Only in their later years were they able to buy a humble house in the older section of Los Angeles where the pastor's ministry ended. But my, they were proud of that house! And the children are two people who know very well the joy and solid foundation of a love that sacrificed for their emergence. Love had honored the gifts and resourced them.

Speaking from our own family experience, Coke and I have known tremendous joy as we have tried to help our four *very* different children discover their unique gifts for their own fulfillment, and for their service in life. How rich it has been to see their interests emerge and grow over the years, and then work to resource the development of each of their specific talents. Honoring their gifts has been one of the major tasks of our marriage. Our three sons are now in graduate school: Dan is in law, Tim in medicine, and Jamie begins seminary next year. Our daughter wants to go into family counseling, but not until she and her husband, Craig, feel their own little family is ready for it. We also have had the privilege of seeing a very gifted minority student through her education. Honoring and helping others develop their gifts is one of the great joys of life. We have often said it seems almost selfish . . . on our part and we have had to ask God to check our motives, as the returns have been so great. In terms of deep and lasting satisfaction, that is absolutely true. Love supports and helps others' gifts to grow.

6 Sexuality:
God's Good Gift

by Coke

by Coke

Genesis makes it wonderfully clear that sexuality is God's idea, and He has told us it is *very* good. All through Scripture, the health and rightness of sex is sustained. Any lack of health, or sinfulness in the expression of our sexuality, is not due to the way God created us, but to the way we might misuse what He has created. The fact that sex is a gift from God is undisputable, and He does not give evil gifts. Only as we abuse it, does it become less than the lovely expression God means for it to be.

But our society seems to be *obsessed* with sex. Dr. Rollo May says we put "more emphasis on sex than any society since that of ancient Rome" (*Love and Will*, Norton, p. 39). But sadly our society focuses on the *abuses* of sex, rather than the beauty of God's gift in marriage. Movies and TV soap operas innundate us with wave upon wave of extramarital affairs, incestuous relationships, and every possible form of sexual abuse. How rare it is to see the excitement and beauty of sex portrayed in the lives of healthy, committed couples.

I really feel like getting on a soapbox and saying, "Listen, fellows, you've got it all wrong. You keep talking about sex *outside* of marriage as though that's the only kind worth talking about. I think the reverse is true. Sex within the context of a *total* relationship with commitment and trust as a base, is where the real action is! There two people can grow together in the deepest and most revealing intimacy possible, and *real* union can take place. And *that* is really exciting!"

But down from my soapbox and back to what Scripture has to say.

The Bible takes sex very seriously, and affirms it as deep, bonding, costly, ministering, and tremendously fulfilling emotionally. From the biblical viewpoint, sex is a celebration of love and life.

Furthermore, the Scriptures tell us that sex is not something we "do"; sex is *part* of us (Ecc. 9:9; Song of Solomon). We are sexual beings with the ability to express our sexuality in different ways. This is not an accident. Each expression has a purpose.

The first purpose that comes to my mind is that of bonding and oneness. In Genesis 2:24 we read: "Therefore a man leaves his father and mother and cleaves to his wife, and they become one flesh." For me, this command to be "one flesh" is as significant as the command to be fruitful and multiply."

Oneness—how much a part of God's good purpose it is. Yet there are conditions to oneness. In the more traditional marriage services, a question is asked: Will you pledge your troth to _____? As they answer "yes," the couple promises to enter into a unique and exclusive relationship that includes, among other things, sexual fidelity.

In a Christian marriage faithfulness is expected of both husband and wife. Old-fashioned? Perhaps. Sensible? Definitely! For only when fidelity is their lifestyle can two peole know the freedom and trust that enable them to express their love completely. In Proverbs, the writer warns us about the misuse of sexual life, and then in lovely, positive words of admonition, speaks of faithfulness: "Drink water from your own cistern, flowing water from your own well.... Let your fountain be blessed, and rejoice in the wife of your youth" (5:15-18). When two people are blessed with this kind of oneness and uniqueness in their marriage, it does not turn them inward to their own private world. Quite the opposite happens. It seems to me they are more able to share their partners with life and other people, without jealousy or possessiveness, precisely because they *know* they have a holy, private place where they belong to each other alone. In this place they know the full and free expression of their love. It is there that they are refreshed and renewed, enabled to go out to other people and to the world. Not only they, but others are blessed by their faithfulness to the vows they made at the altar.

Sexual oneness, as God planned it, is experienced by people who feel they belong to each other in a larger sense, by two people who really care about each other as persons and are committed to sharing all of life.

Of course, even within faithful relationships, there are endless ways to stifle unity and oneness in sex and to sin against the spirit of our partner by a shabby attitude. If a husband or wife comes home from work, mumbles some unintelligible greeting, eats without a word, and then hides behind the newspaper or a current bestseller until bedtime, he or she cannot expect a mate to turn into a passionate partner just because they get into bed together. Sex, as God designed it, is *union*, not simply orgasmic release. Sex doesn't begin in the bedroom—*it permeates all of life.* It is an act that belongs in the context of a total relationship. For in our sexuality we express the quality of our everyday life, and when two people have lost touch with each other in the simple things, they may find themselves resisting sexual intimacy because it has no everyday love to express.

Another very important part of oneness is submission.

Sexual unity calls for the *ultimate* in mutual submission, as two people present themselves to each other, accepting each other just as they are. It is a test of trust, one that, in the beginning, requires courage for total unmasking of body and soul. For oneness means giving up the very personal and private you. This kind of submission is not easy. For some it is much harder than for others; yet it is well worth the abandonment of self that it requires. Unless two people can *both* surrender to the other, and also *both* be willing to be initiators, they will miss some of the specialness and oneness God has created for them.

Another of the great purposes of sex is procreation: "And God blesed them, and God said to them, 'Be fruitful and multiply, and fill the earth and subdue it'" (Gen. 1:28). The conception of a child is the most explicit way in which two people become one. And yet children are not to become an extension of a parental ego. Each child is a unique creation and has a particular destiny to fulfill. He or she should never be expected to live out someone else's unfulfilled dreams.

As I think about sex for the purpose of procreation, I am wondering about the aura in which the act of conception takes place. In our society we take very seriously the way in which a person dies. But the way in which a person begins life is equally important. Are the parents committed to each other? Are they committing themselves to the child? Is conception a fear or a hope?

I also wonder, now that we are aware of the spiraling rise in world population and of the many human beings who die every day of malnutrition or hunger, if it isn't time for us to exercise our procreative responsibility in a new way. For generations we have done well at filling the earth. Perhaps now it is time for us to submit to the *limits* of our earth. Of course, that's easy for me to say, now that I've had the four children I've always wanted. I can just hear our oldest son, who is our family ecology and population expert, say, "Nice going, Mom. How'd you manage that? Four kids in five years!" What he means is, I'd have a hard time justifying myself if I were having our children now, and he's right. Discovering the best way to exercise Christian responsibility in this area is a task my generation has left to his.

Communication is another purpose of sex, and one that is strongly supported in Scripture: "Now Adam *knew* Eve his wife" (Gen. 4:1, author's italics).

The deepest human need is to be *known* and *loved.* Certainly not for all, but for most people, the potential fulfillment of that need is found in the close and covenanted relationship of husband and wife. Communication—knowing and being known in depth—is one of the greatest joys of sex and of marriage itself. When a marriage has *soul*, and two people are growing together in their total relationship, there are moments of union that transcend both word and touch. Call it "mystical," if you wish. That's what Paul called it; a "mystery" (*musterion*) (Eph. 5:32)—a beautiful union that has significance and meaning far beyond the physical act. It is sharing not only the body, but the life of another. It is not an everyday occurrence, nor does it need to be. But once it happens, it leaves its mark not only on the marriage but on all of the couple's life.

The psychiatrist Abraham Maslow has found that, in self-actualizing people, love and sexual satisfaction improve with the age of the relationship. I like that! It confirms my belief—as does Paul Tournier's *Growing Old*, and Dr. Robert Butler's *Sex in the Sixties*—that all of God's relationships operate according to the law of increasing returns.

Some people look upon sex in older people as somehow abnormal, but apparently there is no reason for this. In fact, there is much data to confirm the fact that a healthy, if not as active, sex life can continue all through life. Old people seem to be more reserved in speaking about it, but doctors who work in geriatrics tell us this is so.

Dr. Tournier says: "With age there is established a more harmonious equilibrium among the three factors in conjugal love, namely, the physical, the sentimental, and the spiritual; whereas in the young the first tends to eclipse the other two" (*Learn to Grow*, Harper & Row, p. 95).

Of course, ill health and other unavoidable hindrances can get in the way for periods of time. Still, a couple who knows oneness can feel optimistic about the effect of the passing years on their sexual life.

We know a couple who most certainly confirm this expectation. Ken and Hilda were in their early sixties when we were in our twenties, and naturally we felt that sex was invented for people of our age. How wrong we were! One day Hilda took me aside and said, "Oh, Coke, since Ken has retired, we've been having so much fun! We have time to do things we've wanted to do for years." She giggled, "We even go roller-skating! And our sex life! Well, it's never been so good!" Isn't that wonderful! I gave Hilda a big hug because I felt so happy for her, and for me, because she had expanded my limited idea of what happens to sex in later years.

Ken and Hilda are in their eighties now, and the miles separate us from them. But the picture and message on their Christmas card each year assure us that life is still very capable of producing a bright twinkle in their eyes!

If good sex is based on the fulfillment of needs, then all the years a couple have lived together should increase their level of sensitivity to the things that please each other. Therefore, the communication that is part of sex should get better as time goes on.

When a man and woman marry, they *do* commit themselves to minister to each other's needs. That is another purpose of sex made clear in the Scriptures. Paul tells us that the husband does not own his body . . . his wife does. Conversely, the wife's body is not hers, but his (1 Cor. 7:3-5).

People differ, marriages differ, and so, of course, do needs. There are great variations between couples when it comes to how intense, how frequent, how anything else their sexual expression should be. For these facets of sex there are no rules. Each couple must be in touch with their own needs. But there are ways in which their concern for each other enables, even urges, them to minister to each through their sexual relationship. Paul, in fact, says in marriage it is a "fraud" not to *minister* to each other in this way (1 Cor. 7:5).

It seems to me that Christian husbands and wives especially owe it to one another to take their sexual responsibilities seriously. Well, on second thought, not *so* seriously that it can't be fun, but seriously enough to be really important and to merit undivided attention. Often when I think of the attitude surrounding sex, the verse, "Whatsoever you do, do with all your heart" (Ecc. 9:10, author's paraphrase) flashes across my mind. For what is more dismal than the thought of a halfhearted lover—a husband going through amorous motions while thinking of an upcoming sales meeting, or a wife planning the menu for a dinner party while giving her husband his conjugal rights. Much of the thrill and joy of sex begins right between the ears—in our minds, in our powers of concentration, and in our ability to give ourselves to this God-given expression of love "with all [our] heart."

Of course, there are obstacles to this kind of wholehearted giving in sex; they come to everyone at times. We have mentioned illness, and there is that archenemy of sex—fatigue. Hopefully these would last only a season and would be valid reasons, not masked excuses, to avoid closeness. When someone uses these circumstances as excuses over a long period of time, there is real danger to the marriage. The person may want love and fidelity but at the same time is closing the door to a very important expression of closeness and intimacy in which love and fidelity can grow.

Another obstacle to wholehearted giving is busyness. Sex was not meant to be crowded into the tiny bits of time when a couple is least able to enjoy it. Of course, there will be those unexpected brief encounters, but they should not become the norm. Sex cannot remain healthy and nourished while feeding continually from the crumbs off the table. When we are too busy to find time to express our love, we are *indeed* too busy!

Problems can also take a man and a woman away from each other sexually, and although sex is reconciling, it should not take the place of honestly and openly facing our problems. Sex is not an *escape*. It releases tension, and that is a *good* gift, but it is meant to set us up for life, not to take us from it.

However, once we have dealt with the problems in our relationship, there is no question that a time of lovemaking can be healing beyond words. I like the way Frederick Buechner puts it:

> Contrary to Mrs. Grundy, sex is not sin.
> Contrary to Hugh Hefner, it's not salvation
> either. *Like nitroglycerin, it can be used*
> *either to blow up bridges or heal hearts*
> (*Wishful Thinking*, Harper & Row, p. 87).

The last purpose of sex I see stressed in Scripture is the golden thread of joy and pleasure that runs through every other purpose. It is worthy and beautiful in itself. Once again, no two couples are alike, and there are no rules as to how each is to find pleasure. Whatever brings two people joy and a sense of well-being is right for them; and when that rightness is affirmed again and again as it is when the couple are together sexually, they are people deeply blessed. In poetic, symbolic language,

Proverbs speaks often of the pleasure and joy of love-making ... "Let your fountain be blessed, and *rejoice* in the wife of your youth, a lovely hind, a graceful doe. Let her affection fill you at all times with *delight*, be infatuated always with her love" (5:18-19). "My beloved put his hand to the latch, and my heart was *thrilled* within me" (Song 5:4, author's italics).

Rejoice ... *delight* ... *thrill* ... words of pleasure and joy ... *biblical words* that put us in touch with ourselves as sexual beings and help to free us to enjoy our humanity and our spirituality. For part of our praise to God is in our wholehearted and liberated celebration of sex, and in our "guiltless gratitude" to Him for His good and beautiful gift.

7 Consensus or Consequences:
Religion, Sex, and Children

by Louie

It happened again, just the other day. A couple married for several years came in for counseling. They wanted to save their marriage; yet they were beginning to think they never should have married in the first place. Neither was living up to the other's expectations. Each one had become someone "different from what I had imagined." In a sense, the more they knew of one another, the more they became strangers.

I'm not sure that love is blind, but infatuation certainly is. In the early stages of a romantic relationship a man and a woman can be so caught up in the excitement of a new personality and in the sexual attractions they feel, that they don't see each other clearly. Sometimes they create an image of the other person, and then marry the image rather than the real person. Illusion pushes reality out of the picture.

The romantic attraction can keep you from knowing the real person. That is why courtship is important. It is not a useless ritual, nor should it be a period of enforced frustration.

Ideally, courtship should allow a couple to work their way through the blur of infatuation toward the sharper focus of reality. This is their opportunity to get to know one another as best they can. And, more importantly, this is that critical time when they decide whether or not they are ready to close the door on options, and focus in on a lifelong commitment.

My counseling experience has taught me that there are some basic areas in which a man and woman need to agree if they are to have a quality marriage. I have chosen seven areas to discuss in this chapter and the next: religion, sex, children, finance, friends, home, and goals. Because these areas arouse such strong feelings in all of us, I feel a couple will be in for trouble if they basically disagree on many of them.

When infatuation ends, a couple must live in these areas of reality. How sad it is if their discovery of one another becomes a disappointment, a sudden shattering of the fantasy each had built around the other. And how much better if a couple can reveal themselves as honestly and courageously as they are able to before making a lifelong commitment. This may be difficult, but it is part of becoming mature. The pain of realizing that they have basic differences is better borne before a man and a woman marry. Otherwise they may be crushed by the way the other seems to change later on.

We human beings are always in process of change— and that can work in our favor. When a couple is not completely in agreement about the bases of their relationship as they begin their marriage, they can grow and change together. If they can communicate their ideas and feelings honestly and maturely, the process of change can bring them to new agreements.

The following steps will help you to explore these areas: Set aside a definite period of time to be alone and undisturbed together. Read aloud the section on one area of the seven basics. Then each of you write a "profile of feelings" on that area and compare them with your partner's profile in a spirit of love and honesty.

Each person should try to the best of his or her ability to understand the feelings of the other. This exchange of feelings will stimulate each to become more deeply and realistically acquainted with the other. You are now face-to-face with your agreements and/or differences. How you cope with the differences is going to be a highly individual matter, and you will be influenced by your openness to one another, the depth of your differences, the intensity of your feelings, and the time necessary to make adjustments. If nothing else comes of this time together, you are certainly going to be more truly aware of one another.

Religion

Religion arouses the deepest emotions of the human personality. Even those who look down their noses at religion usually are the first to say that it has been the cause of some of man's bitterest wars.

Bring a strong difference of religion into a marriage, where both husband and wife have had significant religious conditioning, and there is indeed the makings for war. If, on the other hand, one or both of the couple has had no particular depth of feeling about religion, any differences will probably be mild and cause little irritation.

Why all the emotion about religion?

The answer lies in the *meaning* of religion. The word means "that to which one is bound." Religion, therefore, is that to which we are tied or bound, determining what we live for; it indicates our direction and determines our priorities. In the long run, our deepest motivations are determined by religion. It is religion that shapes our lives.

What do *I* mean by *religion*? Religion is that for which you will give up other things in life.

What will *you* give up other things for? What is the one thing you will *not* give up for anything else? I usually ask young couples I am counseling for marriage to try this exercise: Elbow out some time, curl up with each other, and share whatever it is that is most important to you. That will help you begin to see what you are bound to.

Now, what was it—security, family, money, your home, position, success, influence, community status, God, Jesus Christ and His kingdom?

Did your religions agree?

If not, hang on to your hat, because unless some sort of agreement can be reached, each of you will be tugging madly in different directions for the control of the limited resources of your lives: time, money, energy, and affection. And because the motivations are so primal, these tugs of war could create tensions that will be more than your marriage can handle.

Suppose one of you wishes to give large amounts of time, energy, or money to Christ's work and the church, but the other wants those same resources spent on the social scene, the country club, and the business ladder. In spite of your compromises, you will miss the thrill of unity, and very likely you will experience a rift of emotions.

Religion is a growing experience, and the growth demands a means of expression. Now it's true that we know some couples where both partners have a deep personal faith in Christ, and though they worship in different traditions they still have a real sense of spiritual oneness in their home and marriage. However, couples such as this, in my experience, are the exceptions. Generally, if a couple cannot *go* together to church, they most likely will not *grow* together spiritually. And that will be a serious loss!

The other night Colleen and I attended a party where we met the charming wife of a young professional man. She had just had a very real religious experience that had made some considerable changes in her life and feelings. Her husband did not attend church with her. He left her and their children to "do their religious thing" which, I felt he thought was for "little old ladies and children and not red-blooded American men." The wife's pain and sense of loneliness were marked and rather tragic. Something which for many couples had been a bonding, deepening influence had become a point of raised eyebrows and ridicule in their marriage. This is one of the most painful and damaging interactions that can strike a couple's relationship.

Some couples, sensing their deep difference in religion, try to make deals or strike compromises. "Dr. Evans, we have it all worked out. On one Sunday we'll go to his church, on the other Sunday we'll go to my church. We'll let the children make up their own minds when they come of age."

Some deal! First of all, neither one can really put his or her heart into the religion of his or her choice, because that would put too much strain on the other. The agreement has hobbled both in their religious growth, and when something does not grow it becomes stagnant. The couple also have put their children in a very awkward position. First, they will ask their children to choose one denomination over another without having much orientation in either. Another burden is that when they ask the children to choose one of their churches, it is much like asking them to choose between Mom and Dad. And what child wants to do that? Usually the children do nothing, walk off into a religious wasteland, and raise their children as little pagans. By this time the religion that once was somebody's experience has become a convention, then an inconvenience, and finally totally irrelevant—all because of a "deal." Thank God, many young people sense the bankruptcy of such agreements and take seriously their religious commitments, being mature enough to grapple with the meaning of difference early in the game.

In some marriages where there is strong disagreement about religion one of the couple converts. Usually this happens when one partner feels very strongly about his or her faith and the other, sensing this and not having strong feelings of his or her own, says, "OK, I'll convert." Sometimes it is an honest conversion, and the couple knows the joy of real religious unity in their marriage. Great! But in too many instances the scene goes something like this: Party A converts to Party B's religion—and unconsciously slips a card up his or her sleeve. Years go by. Then comes a struggle over a decision where apparently someone is going to have to give in. Slowly Party A's hand goes up the sleeve and pulls out the trump card. "Remember when I converted to your religion? Now it is your turn to convert to my opinion!" Usually this is not agreeable to Party B, who considers it both unfair and irrelevant. It is!

Sometimes one of the partners agrees to raise the children in the other's faith. Once I was called into a gorgeous home overlooking the Pacific Ocean from the high ridges of Bel Air, California. The wife had been a Roman Catholic, although not a very active one. The husband had been an Episcopalian. They decided to compromise and come to a Presbyterian church. (I still can't see how the Presbyterians stand halfway between the Episcopalians and Roman Catholics!) When their first child was of educable age, the wife suddenly felt deep pangs of guilt for not raising her child in the Roman Catholic faith. Her husband reminded her of her agreement, and I shall never forget the tragic truth of her response: "Yes, but I didn't realize what I was doing."

Of course, she didn't! Intellectually, she had made an agreement, an honest one, but without realizing that the conditioning and training we receive as children find deep roots in the religious furrows of our hearts. Just because we chop off the top portion of the plant and

clear the field by some rational decision does not mean
that the rootstock is dead. It may still be very active and
able to come strongly to life under the right conditions.
The religious training of the children was all the stimu-
lation this woman's roots needed.

When faith is a matter of agreement, it is the most
unifying and healing power a marriage can have. A
husband and wife who know Christ sense their acceptance by God as the Holy Spirit pours into their lives. It
undergirds them with a deep sense of security, and several things happen. First, they both receive a basic affirmation from God's own Spirit, which gives them an
assurance of acceptance by Someone very important to
them. Then, the couple has a powerful Other to whom
they can relate when they have differences. Neither
must come to the place of the other; each can walk to a
higher third position. As they come closer to Christ,
they come closer to each other.

Years ago, when Colleen and I lived in Los Angeles,
we occasionally got tickets to the Rose Bowl game. We
loved to park our car on the golf course, eat a picnic
lunch with friends, and then walk over to the stadium.
I would always give Coke her ticket so that if we got
separated in the jostling crowd, we could end up at the
same place. I would always say, "Honey, in case we get
separated, I'll meet you at tunnel so-and-so."

Once we *did* get separated! For a moment I felt waves
of anxiety come over me as I found myself muttering,
"What am I going to do now?" Then my last words to
Colleen rang in my ears: "I'll meet you at tunnel so-and-
so." When I got to the tunnel I stood on tiptoe, craning
my neck to look over the crowd in hopes of finding
Coke. There she came, pushed and shoved by the fast-
moving crowd, smiling at those who apologized for
bumping into her, her hand raised to hold her little
knitted cap on her head. We had ended up at the same
place.

When a Christian couple get separated by differences of opinion, each can always say, "Honey, I'll meet you at the feet of Christ." Neither has to come to the place of the other; nobody has to "win" or be right. Instead, each makes whatever corrections are necessary to bring him or her to the feet of Christ, and the closer they come to Him, the closer they come to one another.

Sex

A couple I know always tells sex-oriented jokes. However, in private counseling sessions, the wife told me she thought intercourse was "the goring of an innocent victim." Unable to find satisfaction in her relationship with her husband, she constantly tries to bring other men and women together, often without regard for their marital status. Disruption follows in her wake all too many times. If this woman and her husband could have talked out their feelings about sex prior to their marriage, perhaps they could have done something about her unfortunate attitude. But to have talked about such things would have been improper in the sexual atmosphere in which this couple was raised.

I do not feel it is at all improper for a couple in their maturing relationship to talk about sex and its meaning to each of them. I would hope they would ask each other such questions as, "What was the sexual atmosphere of your home? How do you think your mother and father felt about sex? In what ways did they indicate their joy or embarrassment about it? How did you come to know 'the facts of life'?" (The answer to that last question might be good for some real laughs.)

My first awareness of sex with Colleen was characterized by a deep sense of communication. Having both experienced a new relationship with Christ, we gave our new relationship with each other to Him. He would have us "save ourselves" for marriage, and we knew that would take all the strength we had—and more—so we determined to lean heavily on God and accept from Him the "strength for all things" He has promised. We wanted our physical expression to be an honest manifestation of our total relationship. We did not want to allow the sexual expressions to get out in front of the total relationship, nor did we want them to lag behind. (I must say, the latter was far easier than the former!) We felt that when we were ready "to go all the way" we would "go all the way in *every* way," which meant marriage vows. We did not want our relationship to boomerang later with a false sense of obligation.

As I counsel couples in midlife who are having difficulties, I discover a surprising number of cases in which one or the other feels that he or she was forced into the marriage. When we get down to specifics, it turns out to have been premarital intercourse that resulted in a sense of belonging and therefore of obligation.

Of course some people say, "Just remove the cultural conditioning of obligation that goes along with intercourse, then we will be free to enjoy the relationship without hang-ups."

That seems fine in theory, if we can accept the possibility that intercourse has no inherent bonding characteristics. But suppose it *does*. Then no deculturization will ever remove the deep feeling of belonging two people have when they share such a powerful, beautiful experience. This feeling of belonging is exactly what the Scriptures teach, and what many cultures through the ages have taught (1 Cor. 6:15-20). It is an almost universal human understanding.

But back to the concept of intimate communication in sexual relationships. In sexual intercourse, two persons completely bare themselves to one another, not only physically, but emotionally and personally in the deepest sense. In this act two persons "become one flesh," and in the Hebrew understanding of the word, that was not just a fleshly or physical union, but one involving the total personality. It was under the Greek influence that we thought we could divide the human personality into segments. But each of us is an integrated whole, and one part of our personalities interacts constantly with the other parts; they never can function separately. Thus the psyche and covenant factors of our personalities are involved with the sexual. That is why when a convenience relationship comes to an end, one or both persons feel exploited.

To put it another way, the total personality is like a plant, with sex as the flower. Cut the flower from the stem and the roots, and it soon withers. Cut sex from the total relationship of life, and it cannot hold two persons together. In fact it becomes stale, even objectionable.

The plant of the total relationship is made up of the stem of covenant, the leaves of common commitments and basic agreements, the roots of spiritual commitment, and the soil of social and religious heritage. When the whole plant is strong, the blossoms of sexual joy actually multiply and become more exciting and fragrant with the years!

Of course, sexual relationships do not always culminate in intercourse. At times, a quiet closeness between husband and wife can be an exquisite, relaxing form of refreshment. "Tactile tenderness," "cutaneous contact," or "Vitamin S [for skin]," when mixed with hours of sharing and conversation, can leave a couple alive with a glowing sense of unity.

By all means, talk about sex before marriage. Get help from a professional if you need it. Your agreement or disagreement can make the difference between the experience of oneness or the agony of a division that grows wider with each passing year.

Children

What are children? A foolish question? Not really. It is a very basic question. Is a child only a social responsibility? If so, he will not feel that his parents take a delight in him.

Is a child an extension of our own ego? I certainly hope not. A child may have some characteristics of mother and father, but the child is a unique creation, a totally individual combination of strengths and weaknesses. He or she is not here to duplicate Aunt So-and-So or Grandfather Such-and-Such. Each child is a special creation for whom God has a plan, and the task of the parents is to help that child find out who he or she is without seriously tampering with the results.

One of the first questions a couple usually asks is: How many children should we have, if any? Are we only to replace ourselves, or disregard zero population growth? I know one young couple who "refuse to bring a child into the maelstrom of hatred we call life on earth." Other questions follow: How do we feel about birth control, and by what methods? Under what circumstances, if any, would we agree upon abortion?

Would we consider children to be an inconvenience, and if so, when? Only in the early part of the marriage, or all through it? And what would be inconvenienced—travel, career, personal freedom, social life?

What fears do we have regarding children? That we won't be up to the job of raising them? Childbirth itself? Genetic deformity? Financial incapability? Fear of world cataclysm?

Who is going to take care of the children? Is that the wife's job, or does the father get into the act as well? If he does, how and with what responsibilities?

What will be our standards of discipline? Will we stand together, or will the little rascal wedge in between us? If we disagree on a given matter of discipline, how will we handle it? Does a mother tell the children, "When Daddy comes home, you are going to get a spanking"? Or do we operate on the basis of whoever sees the misbehavior administers the discipline?

Perhaps one of the most important questions is, Who is more important—my spouse or the children?

I hope it will be your mate. After all, he or she is the one you will live with before the children come, and what you have together is what you are left with after the children are gone. Moreover, if children sense that they can drive a wedge between their parents, believe me, the plans are already being made! But when a child senses that Mom and Dad are together and unshakable, he or she may have moments of frustration because the child can't work one against the other, yet that very frustration will turn into a sense of security and certainty. "If I can't drive them apart, nothing can."

And one last question might be: What gifts does each of us bring to the rearing of our children? Above all, I hope your children will feel that they are a delight to you both. Nothing prepares a person for life better than knowing they make people happy.

We had gone over to the Taylors' home one evening for dinner. They were the kind of folks who were a joy to be around—no airs, and ample love for everybody, including their little son Josh. Most of the early evening Josh roamed around the room, checking in on each guest and getting love from different ones. Then the baby-sitter took him upstairs, got him ready for bed, and allowed him to come down one last time to say good night to everyone. He toddled around in his "Doctor Dentons," giving everybody a kiss and a hug. Then his daddy gave him a loving pat on his bottom, and he headed toward the stairs. I couldn't help calling after him, "Good night, Josh—we love you!"

He kept right on going, concentrating on lifting his stubby little legs over those big stairs, but he called back, "I love me too!"

What a great way for a child to feel! And having received love, he will be able to give love.

8 Mutuality or Misery: Finances, Friends, Home, and Goals

by Louie

During the days of the open housing controversy, I had preached on several occasions on the theme of our oneness in Christ, and therefore the oneness we had in communal relations. Subsequently, a black family enrolled their child in the Sunday School. After one of the services, I heard a commotion in the courtyard and, stepping toward the action, was suddenly confronted by a man who saw me and bolted from the crowd. As he approached, he deliberately reached into his back pocket, pulled out his wallet, and waved it under my nose. He was a vocal Christian, highly successful in his business and living in a sumptuous house in one of the finest sections of the city. With irate intensity, he fairly shouted, "Louis Evans, I like you, but if what you do in this church lowers my property value by one dime, I'll fight you up and down the streets!" Apparently, I had threatened his god.

Finances
What is money? Every couple should know. And yet, sometimes it goes so fast we might answer that question by half jesting and half crying, "I wish I knew! I

don't see enough of it to know!"

In all seriousness, we need to ask the question, and we need to arrive at an operational agreement.

Is money our *summum bonum*—our highest goal?

Is money our basis of security?

Or, turn the question around. What will we do for money, and what will we *not* do for money?

What is the importance of money and material possessions in our marriage? Money means *something* to all couples. What does it mean to us?

Many couples are confronted with a dilemma by Christ's words: "No one can serve two masters; for either he will hate the one and love the other, or he will be devoted to the one and despise the other. You cannot serve God and mammon [materialism]" (Matt. 6:24). For those who choose to serve the god of mammon, religion which can outwardly appear to be so important and staunchly defended becomes only a cloak or veneer. It is never allowed to influence the outcome of the money game. And certainly, for these people, it would be unthinkable for religion to encounter or challenge the economic system.

Money is a symbol of life, for it represents our labor and our creative individuality. Money, and the manner in which we use it, communicate a great deal about our personalities. Money is one of the principal ways we express our loyalties and priorities, so that when Christ calls for us to tithe, He very quickly gets a response, one way or the other! How important is God in your giving?

Actually, all Christians should tithe, right off the top of their income. That should be the first check written each month. This is simply a recognition that God is Lord of all of life. "The earth is the Lord's" and we are but using it for a while. If, as a people, we misuse it, the Lord will sooner or later give it to others.

Recently a rather antagonistic middle-aged church member challenged me to give him one good reason why he should tithe. I gave him several, beginning with the one above, and going on to mention the fact that a Christian is one who considers himself a manager or steward for Christ. In His death upon the cross, Christ paid a price for our liberation, and in His Resurrection He gave us the power for new life. We should be deeply grateful *if* we understand and have experienced what Christ has done for us.

Then suddenly an idea came over me. I shot his question back to him, slightly altered: "Give one good reason why you should *not* tithe!" He gave me several, none of them very good. But his reasons told me who his master was, and it was not Christ. It was mammon. His cloak of religiosity had been blown aside which allowed me to see his real uniform underneath.

That same kind of antagonism can erupt in a marriage when a couple does not agree on financial priorities. So, before your marriage—or even after it—it's a good idea to set aside some quiet time to talk over your feelings about money. For instance, who will be in charge? I hope that, although you are conscious of each other's gifts regarding financial management, both of you will accept some of the responsibility for these duties. If not, the "manager" gets all the flak when something goes wrong. Both of you should be in on the budget-making, although each should have some part of the budget he or she administers without constant referral to the other. Moreover, each should have some "mad money" to spend on *anything* desired.

And, please, don't get so deeply in debt that you can't see your way out. Life is too short to spend it at each other's throats, which is where most couples seem to fly when things get tight financially. Money problems stand right near the top of the list as causes for sunken marriages.

Early in our marriage, Coke and I were always bumping our noses into financial dead ends. Either we had an insurance bill to pay or an unexpected repair bill, or Christmas, or vacation would leave us devastated, and me on the verge of panic. "Why punish ourselves this way?" we finally said. "We know we will have to spend those amounts, so why not get ready for them?"

Difficult though it was, we began to lay aside the monies in an accrual account. We added up all the big payments that came due each year, divided the sum by twelve, and had the bank take that amount out of our checking account each month and put it into a savings account. Then, when a bill came due, we simply withdrew the proper amount, put it into our checking account, and paid the bill. We even went out to dinner on the interest on that account! What a relief! True, we're in a slight pinch every month, but it surely beats the panic and the strain that used to upend our relationship.

One of the great joys of managing our money has been dreaming. Right now we are in the process of building a vacation cabin with our own hands in the High Sierra country, and all the family is in on it. We're trying to "go lean" for it, and though the shocking expenses of the college years plague us, we find the dreaming is half the fun! The simplicity a couple achieves while striving toward a dream is one of the most unifying experiences a marriage can have.

What is money? A source of great joy when top priority is given to the Lord and the needs of the world—and the rest fulfills a dream with a purpose.

Friends

Several years ago, a lovely young woman came to Coke and wept out her story of her husband's rudeness to her friends. He thought they were uncouth because they laughed openly, uncultured because they were not well-heeled, and sickeningly sweet because they showed their love for one another with hugs and embraces.

"It hurts me so much," the woman sobbed. "It's not

only that he rejects such neat people—he's also rejecting part of me! I've known and loved these people for years, and they are part of my life!"

She was right. Friends *are* a part of us, and in a marriage it is important for a husband and wife to accept each other's friends. That does not mean they must make them their *best* friends, but it does mean that they should honor their spouse's friendships and those needs the friends fulfill.

I have some flying friends, and some buddies who work on cars with me. Coke has friends with whom she can talk politics or with whom she shares inner-city concerns in our community or involvements such as the Hunger Committee at church. We both give up some segment of time to the other for the development of these friendships.

Then there are those friends we both enjoy. No marriage is sufficient to itself. Each needs elements of an extended family, of persons who have covenanted to be available to us and sensitive to our needs. We call these friends our "warm fuzzies." We don't have to dress up to be with them. We can relax in their presence—even snooze on their couch if we want to!

Sometimes, however, friendships can create problems in marriage. "My best friend" can short-circuit the best-friend relationship that spouses should have with each other. Coke will be talking more about the importance of friendship in marriage in the next chapter.

In the Song of Solomon there is a beautiful expression: "This is my beloved and this is my friend" (5:16). When certain intimate concerns are hidden from one's mate and told to a friend, that indicates one partner's distrust of the other. A husband and wife should be "best friend" to the other—and yet neither can expect a spouse to be all that he or she needs in every segment of life. That puts a tremendous burden on a mate by demanding something he or she cannot give and therefore stimulates those uncomfortable, painful feelings of inadequacy that usually hound most of us.

If one partner says, "I can't make it without you," that puts the other in a straitjacket. It prevents him or her from taking certain kinds of risks that are necessary for a fulfilled life. I'm not talking about foolhardy risks but about those involved with challenges to our creativity and development as a person. Now, true, husbands and wives need one another and should make themselves available for the others' needs. If, however, the other is so dependent that he or she cannot get along even for a short period of time, then the "box" closes in and the prison term begins.

In our opinion, the best marriages are made up of two people who could make it on their own if they had to, who do not clutch at their mate as though he or she were a life preserver in a stormy sea, but who *choose* to be together in mutual submission.

Dependent, independent, and interdependent are three very difficult words. The dependent person rides on the back of another, sucks all strength from the other, and gives little or nothing back. The independent person marches through life proudly and alone, shunning the loving ministry of those around him. But there is a period in which the dependent person must be able to stand on his or her own—not aloof or isolated, but strong, able to manage the affairs of life without whimpering or whining, capable of stepping into the harness and pulling a portion of the load. This makes the person interdependent—someone who gives according to ability and graciously receives according to need, someone who builds up the gifts and abilities of others while receiving their resources at the same time. So it should be between the two "best friends" who come together in a marriage.

At this point we should consider questions relating to friendships: How much time should we spend with our friends outside our marriage? What will we do for friendships, and what will we *not* give up for friendship?

Some marriages become smothered when too many friends eat up too much social time. Colleen and I ran into this phenomenon while I was doing postgraduate work in Scotland. We were aliens in a foreign land, although the Scots were most cordial and warm. With about a hundred Americans doing graduate work, however, it was not surprising that our social calendar was soon overloaded!

Coke was nursing our first child, Dan, at the time, and he would not be rushed with his feeding. One night we tried to hurry the whole process because we were planning to go out, and he felt the tension. Perhaps Coke was putting a little something "extra" into the milk that night. At any rate, Dan put up a howl! I thought I heard the strain of an old gospel song in his rebellion, "I shall not be, I shall not be moved!"

Colleen looked at me and shook her head slowly. "Louie, we're going too fast," she said. "If we aren't smart enough to see it, little Dan is."

I mused quietly for a moment while I continued tying my tie. The early weeks of Dan's infancy had been idyllic. I remembered the red glow of the coal fire as I stoked it to life, the sweet sounds of Dan's nursing, and the quiet talks with Coke. I recalled the serenity of sitting on the loveseat, Dan freshly bathed, powdered, and tucked into his soft pajamas, humping his little back in a slow rhythm, his head on my shoulder as we talked and sang. Soon his little body moved more slowly. I could feel his breathing take on that steady pace, and finally his little hand dropped from my chest and was limp at his side.

We would tuck him into his crib, and go back to the den for a night of study or letter writing until BBC's third program would sign off with those familiar words,

"Good night, good night all, good night."

We had time then to be aware and in touch, but now the hectic pace, so typical of our beloved homeland, started to accelerate, and it was increasingly an unacceptable way of life. The answer was evident. Our social life was threatening the quality of our life together, and it was time for us to declare our independence from it—something we have had to do again and again as what Coke calls "the Barrenness of a too busy life" has plagued us down through the years.

Home

When a couple discusses the kind of home they would like to have when they are married, there are two important things to remember: (1) They shouldn't let the home run them, and (2) Neither should they run away from their home. *Home is the basic building block of society.* Home is the place where we interact in such a way that our personalities are shaped and we emerge as individuals. Here we find security. Home contains the necessary elements that help us to live as human beings. Therefore it has to be given a high priority within our whole pattern of life. We cannot allow our careers, our professional and educational interests, our social or community obligations to keep us out of touch with our home. If we do, we will not have the energy, the confidence, or the resources to carry out those other commitments.

A home runs us when we put too much emphasis on its cost, size, location, furnishings, etc. I suppose most couples, at one time or another, take on too much of a house, as we did, and find that it runs them instead of the other way around. Years ago we got a terrific buy—a large, beautiful house with a spacious yard, for a very low price. But keeping it up was something else. It took Dan and Tim three hours to cut the grass, and they were at the age when they had more interesting things to do.

Then we had to put in shrubs and trees, which not only were expensive, but had to be cut and trimmed regularly. We didn't have nearly enough furniture for so much interior space, nor could we afford to go out and buy more. Our car was getting old, and we couldn't afford to replace it because every penny was going into the house.

I was upset at everyone because the house was upsetting me! And not just financially, although as Coke pointed out earlier in the book, that, too, was a disaster. Beautiful as it was, we finally decided, "Who needs it?" We sold it and bought a much smaller house with a charming but maintainable little piece of land. In fact, one summer we vacationed at home and added on to that little house, with all the family involved in drawing plans, framing, shingling, plastering, painting, and decorating. We learned a great deal working together and even now, the children look back on that vacation as a very special time.

A couple should also agree on how their home will be used. Is it for family only, a place secluded from the world, or is it open to others?

I was brought up to think of the home as a place where people were to be made welcome. I'm glad Coke agreed with that, or we could have been in real trouble. Our first Thanksgiving as husband and wife found us living in a tiny basement apartment just off our seminary campus. "How about inviting a couple of the seminarians who don't have families?" Colleen suggested. I concurred, and before we knew it the list had grown to eight. We borrowed a table from the seminary, some folding chairs, and filled the tiny front room/study with happy students and even a visiting professor. And that set the mold. Thereafter our house always seemed to be the place for gatherings, large or small.

One night recently our son Jim recalled his memories of our Bel Air living room, filled with charter members of the new church. He remembered the singing, studying, laughing, and the praying. At times the laughter was so enticing that the children would crawl out into the hall where they could hear but not be seen, and then they would fall asleep on the floor. I'm thankful our children look back and remember our busy home (often hectically so) with warmth and smiles.

In some cases a family comes and goes without any sort of coordinated schedule or agreement regarding the time they spend together. Each person is off in a different direction according to his or her own timetable. "I'm tired of serving dinner three or four times a night," one mother complained. "But what can I do? I can't let my kids live on snacks."

Here is one place where I would stand and fight. Someone needs to take the initiative in getting the family to set aside the dinner hour for family time. Other activities are like respectable thieves we allow into our lives until there is no time left for the family to sit down together and share life—no time to share experiences, plans, pains, hopes, or struggles. Gradually, invisible barriers will begin to separate them, and soon they will feel like strangers in one another's presence. Should any *outside* force so threaten a family, the whole country would be up in arms, yet we often give up by default what we would give our lives to defend.

I am glad Colleen puts her foot down about dinner time. If too many "emergencies" keep me from those moments with my family, I hear about it! And rightly so.

Goals

Do you have a good marriage? If you answer, "Yes, I surely do!" then I have another question. By what criterion do you judge your marriage to be a success? Included among the most frequent responses I receive is "being happy." I'm sure this point of view is encouraged by our society's obsession with pleasure and instant gratification, and at first glance happiness as a goal of marriage sounds reasonable enough. But I have learned that when it is a goal rather than a by-product of other factors, a couple becomes increasingly incapable of dealing with unhappy or painful circumstances. Instead of meeting problems head-on, they look for escape routes, denying themselves those lasting victories and discoveries of strength that come from leaping into the arena of life and honestly struggling with the issues. But who is going to struggle with *un*happiness if happiness is the goal? Such a relationship degenerates into shallow pleasure-seeking, leaving behind a trail of unresolved debris that eventually overwhelms one or both partners.

We cannot seek happiness for its own sake. Happiness is the product of clear agreements, honest struggles, and creative cooperation. Happiness is two people striding together through the routines of life's flatlands, slogging through some deep valleys, and climbing laboriously to mountaintops whose vistas make all the trekking worthwhile. The greatest joys come after some of the most difficult struggles. For joy is not the absence of pain, but the presence of God in the midst of all of life.

Goals have little to do with how we make our living— and a great deal to do with *motivation* and what we are living for. Some couples are motivated to reach for a high position in a corporation, and everything is sacrificed to that. Some want to be included in prestigious society, whereas others strive for political power in their community, state, or nation. Great ambitions can consume a family's time and energy to the point where each member becomes starved for personal attention. The "best" schools and "anything you want" are poor substitutes for the presence, concern, and support of a family member.

Other couples tell me that one of their goals is to grow together, to help one another become all that he or she can be. There are few things more satisfying than to see one we love reaching his or her full potential. To hold another up on hands of prayer, to support her with all the resources we can muster, to watch her touch the stars of her dreams, sends a thrill of delight through a lover's heart.

Some couples say clearly and simply their goal is to live for Christ. They want to do all they can to build His kingdom, using whatever gifts they have for His glory.

What a vast variety of goals there are and how radically they differ! Sadly, couples often come together in the excitement of romance and infatuation and never bother to talk over this most vital area. How many of us have pulled back the curtain of our lives and revealed the deep yearnings that determine what we seek most? It's so important to do, and if these goals and yearnings agree, then two persons have a good chance of experiencing a glorious companionship that gets better with time.

Remember, all God's relationships are designed to operate on the law of increasing returns; they improve with age! So much so that at times we will ask ourselves if we can contain the joy. The answer is "No!" It will simply have to spill over onto others.

Happy is the couple who chooses as their highest priority in life to "Seek . . . first the kingdom of God and His righteousness" (Matt. 6:33, KJV). While happiness is *not* what they seek, it will be theirs as a natural by-product of the high and holy goal they share.

9 Keeping the Glow:
Friendship, Fidelity, and Romance

by Coke

The royal wedding of Prince Charles and Lady Diana in England can surely be called "The Wedding of the Century." Yet it was not all pomp and pageantry. For on that occasion, Robert Runcie, the Archbishop of Canterbury, gave a deep and splendid homily:

> Here is the stuff of which fairy tales are made, the prince and princess on their wedding day. But fairy tales usually end at this point with the simple phrase, "They lived happily every after." This may be because fairy tales regard marriage as an anticlimax after the romance of courtship. This is not the Christian view. Our faith sees the wedding day as a place where the adventure really begins.

He then said,

> Those who are married live happily ever after if they persevere in the real adventure, which is the royal task of creating each other and creating a more loving world.

The "real adventure" is worked out in the arena of a lifelong, committed relationship. And where does romance fit into all of this?

Well, first of all, many of us have to get rid of a lot of unrealistic romantic expectations we have for marriage—the idea of two people meeting and after the most flimsy courtship, riding off in the moonlight to live happily ever after. We laugh, yet that kind of thinking may be more a part of us than we like to admit.

Marriage is the most demanding of all our human relationships, but it also has the greatest potential. When a couple decides together that their relationship is worth real effort, the rewards will be eminently worth it. *Then*, as a result of the true *work* of marriage, they *will* have a sense of romance—not the "riding off in the moonlight" nonsense, but the very real kind that glows with commitment, depth, and sincerity.

It is true that in our society today this kind of marriage is so rare it's considered an oddity, almost a subversive activity. In the words of Oscar Wilde, "The world has grown suspicious of anything that looks like a happy marriage." But psychology tells us that what we are suspicious of is often what we yearn for most deeply. I think that is true. The world yearns to see strong models of marriages that are really working, where commitment, and, yes, romance are very much alive.

This chapter will deal with keeping that glow in our relationship—first, the glow of friendship, then the importance of fidelity, and finally, romance—in that order because, in my opinion, you can forget romance if you are not first friends who treat one another with fidelity and respect.

Friendship

Being married does not mean we do not have other wonderful friendships in our lives, but there is something very special about having a spouse who is best friend, as well as lover. Friendship in marriage can be such a deep and satisfying experience, a companionship of equals, with the added spice of the complementation of the sexes.

"The Lord God said, 'It is not good that the man should be alone'" (Gen. 2:18) and so we were created male and female for companionship. God intended friendship as part of marriage. It is hoped that, in addition to the romantic attraction they feel for each other, two people will make a lifelong commitment because there is also a deep friendship between them. That friendship will serve them well, because children are not a part of all marriages. Even when there are children, they come and they go, so that eventually a couple finds themselves alone again. Children can be a great joy, but they were never meant to sustain a marriage. In day-to-day living in the world of prickly beards, hair in rollers, bouts of illness, and cases of the grumps—as well as in the fun and challenge of building a home together—perhaps the thing that will matter most is that two people are real and trusting friends.

If a man and a woman are friends before they marry and their friendship matures during their marriage, there will be no "twenty-year fracture" when their children begin leaving home. Rather, they will find that at last they have the time they have always wanted for each other. What Louie and I have discovered in these last few years is that as our lives overlap and the more traditional lines of definition fall away, there is more companionship for us—a more creative friendship.

What is a friend? A friend is someone you are comfortable with, someone whose company you prefer. A friend is someone you can count on for support and for honesty.

A friend is one who believes in you, someone with whom you can share your dreams. In fact, a real friend is a person you want to share all of life with, and the sharing doubles the joy.

When you are hurting and you can share your struggle with a friend, it eases the pain. A friend offers you safety and trust, and whatever you say will never be used against you.

A friend will laugh with you, but not at you. A friend is fun.

A friend will pray with you . . . and for you.

A friend is someone with whom you can share ideas and philosophies, someone with whom you can grow intellectually. If one marriage partner is growing intellectually and the other is not, then their relationship will be strained. Growing together intellectually is a form of friendship.

My friend is one who hears my cry of pain, senses my struggle, and shares my lows as well as my highs.

When I am troubled, my friend stands not only by my side, but also stands apart, looking at me with some objectivity. My friend does not always say I am right, because sometimes I am not. One of the worst things that can happen in a marriage is for one partner to take the side of the other when that side is invalid. My friend does not do that. When I am wrong my friend tells me.

Now, when my friend does this, I must admit that it's not the happiest time in our relationship. Part of me would rather have him in my corner—whether I'm right or wrong—but another part of me says, "Wait a minute! You know his point is well taken. You did miss some clues. If you continue in your former thinking, you and the others with you are going to get hurt. So don't be proud."

Honesty has to be part of friendship. Sometimes it disrupts the calmness of a marriage, but it pays off in the long run. When my friend challenges my point of view, it helps me to get in touch with my feelings. It also forces me to become more objective about myself.

This is a delicate balancing act in a marriage relationship. If one partner assumes the role of critic, then he or she has not understood. But if he or she can stand a bit apart and at the same time let his or her partner know that he or she is loyal, then friendship becomes an 'art form.

A friend is not primarily a critic. At least, not *my* friend. I know he loves me. And when he stimulates me to think more clearly, he adds strength to our relationship—and to me. If I find that I have to change my way of thinking, then I am free to do it in the privacy of my own counsel. In the presence of my friend, I haven't lost, nor am I ridiculed.

My lover, my friend—this is what a marriage partner should be.

There are other friends in my life, and I value them highly. But only my best friend knows me so intimately. More than anyone else, he recognizes my strengths and accepts my weaknesses with patience. Only he is sensitive to all my moods and vulnerabilities. It is with him that I can become one.

Through him—my husband, my friend—Christ's love comes most powerfully into my life. Some of my deepest needs are voiced in moments of prayer with him. I give thanks to God most earnestly with him and for him.

Fidelity

It is true, of course, that marriage springs from love, but its stability is based not on love, but on fidelity. Fidelity is the ethical element which enhances natural love, and only by its means does the natural become personal. It is therefore the only quality which can guarantee the permanence of the marriage relation (*The Divine Imperative*, trans. Olive Wyon, Westminster Press, pp. 357-8).

I like a thought of Emil Bruner's. It says something I have felt for a long time: Fidelity is *staying power* in marriage. It provides a base of trust and permanence, and I know for me, romance would not have a chance if it did not spring from that solid base.

Physical fidelity is an expression of mental fidelity, or so it should be. But some people are faithful with their bodies in the strict sense, while they play around thoughtlessly with flirtations and fantasies.

It seems to me Jesus said this was dangerous business, when He said that lust was not just involved in the physical act, but in what takes place in the heart and mind (Matt. 5:28).

David and Karen Mains spoke out on this in an interview with *Family Life Today* magazine. They said (in an article titled "In Defense of Mental Fidelity":

(David)
When two people have settled in their minds that 'I am going to love her or him: and they take those vows before God and witnesses, then that puts an end to the practice of comparing. From that day on they are never again to compare. They are to say, "The whole of my affection is given to this woman, and I will not allow myself to think romantically about another."

(Karen)
Not that we say, "I am going to love you and I'm going to love you alone," and then "poof" everything is all right. You and I know that that is ridiculous. But there is a decision that must be made to be faithful mentally. And then when something comes up that is contrary, we have to make a decision as to what we are going to do with that which is contrary and how we are going to act.

For us, this has meant many things. It has meant not fantasizing sexually or romantically about someone besides our marriage partner. I recognize that this goes against the grain of much counseling, but you and I have made a decision to be faithful in that area, and we have a marriage that I will hold up against anyone's. I am not bragging about our marriage; I am just utterly grateful. It has been one that has come with a great deal of work, but I think the basic key has been to decide to be faithful not only with our bodies but with our minds.

(David)
And sometimes we sound a little prudish. Because I will not allow myself to think romantically about someone else, when a thought comes, I refuse the thought. I won't play with the thought. Well, it sounds like we are the old stereotyped, straight-laced people who wear nothing but black. The truth is just the opposite. This decision has given us tremendous freedom so that my relationships with women in terms of the sister, mother thought-patterns are multiple. And those relationships are very meaningful to me. I feel like a free person. I don't have to worry.

(Karen)
And there is a deep well of peace at the center of our marriage relationship upon which we both draw as we relate to a broken world.

I am grateful for Karen's and David's words. I am also grateful for the "deep well of peace" mental fidelity has brought to our marriage. Louie and I regard it as a gift of God, one we have chosen to receive and nurture. Without the security base that trust and fidelity give our marriage, I know I would not be able to give myself to the happy work keeping the glow of romance requires.

Romance
It was a blustery, cold day in Washington. It was also our day off, and a good time to indulge in one of our

favorite treats—an afternoon at the theater. As it turned out, *A Matter of Gravity* was not my choice for the Play of the Year, but Katherine Hepburn made it well worth the price of admission! She was magnificent! As we walked away from the theater in the early evening, I turned on my mind's "instant replay" where I could hear Miss Hepburn deliver certain key lines and relive the delight of her inimitable style.

One line in particular kept coming back again and again. Miss Hepburn was portraying an elderly widow playing hostess to her grandson and his friends, and at one point she was queried by one of the guests about the quality of her marriage. She replied, with great dignity, "My marriage was a triumph! (*Pause.*) But it took *some* doing."

As she spoke the words, a couple who are close friends and were sitting a few rows ahead of us wheeled around to make sure we had grasped that line. And Louie, sitting next to me, gave me an elbow in the ribs. Apparently it was a line with special meaning for all of us, not just for me. For marriage *is* a triumph—at least it *can* be—but, as Miss Hepburn eloquently reminded us, "It takes *some* doing."

Perhaps no aspect of marriage takes more "doing" than that of keeping romance alive. Romance takes time, energy, planning, and creativity. Yes, it's work! But, like seeing Katherine Hepburn in a play, the delightful results make it well worth the price you pay.

Some years ago I read a best-selling book in which the writer suggested that wives ought to greet their husbands at the door at the end of the day dressed in a baby-doll nightie and high heels. Well, I could hardly wait! When Louie came home that night I—no, I didn't. But what I did do was ask him how he'd *feel* if I greeted him that way one night, and he replied, "I'd like the implication, but not the getup."

Then he chuckled. "That sure would be out of character for us! But I could accept a variety of expressions that say, 'I want time with you.' The thing that turns me on is not what you're wearing, it's you as a person—knowing that you desire me, that we desire each other."

Then, after a pause, he added, "Come to think of it, that getup might be just the ticket for some people."

And he's right! If a nightie and high heels work for the woman who wrote that book, and apparently it does, that's great! But it wouldn't be natural for us. There are no rules for keeping romance alive that will work in the same way for everyone. But one thing that romance does require is a periodic planned sharing we might call "quality time"—time for two people to be together in a very private way, doing whatever pleases *them*.

When our children were small, we played a little game for two called "Make a Tunnel." All we did was to cup our hands around our eyes and bring our heads together until our hands touched, forming a tunnel between us. Then we simply looked into one another's eyes, and with everything around us temporarily blocked out of mind and view, we "let the rest of the world go by." The game didn't take much time, just long enough to look deep and feel something warm and satisfying inside. Today I asked Andie, our now-grown daughter, what "making a tunnel" meant to her back then, and she said, "It made me feel secure, warm, close, and very special." I thought to myself, that's what *romance* in a marriage makes you feel—secure, special, and close. So perhaps "quality time"—looking deep into the eyes of the one you love and "making a tunnel" in whatever way pleases you both—is essential to keeping romance alive.

Recently I was talking with a friend whose husband died a year ago, just before his fiftieth birthday. They had known a good marriage, and she misses him and their life together terribly. As we talked, my friend's eyes filled with tears. I don't think I'll every forget what

she said: "He saw me in a way no one else ever had.
And now that the one who thought I was *most* special,
most beautiful, *most* unique, is gone, I just don't feel I'm
as much those things anymore." She was not complain-
ing. She told me she was rich in memories now because
theirs had been a great love, a romance to the end.
Obviously, they had taken time to look deep, to see in
each other what no one else could see, and to feel warm
and secure in their love. However a couple achieves it,
this is "quality time."

We know several couples who seem to be especially
successful at keeping the glow glowing. Each couple has
their own interpretation of quality time, determined by
their personalities and lifestyle.

Dee and Bill Brehm, for instance, from whom we borrowed the term "quality time," are extremely busy people. Bill has been the Assistant Secretary of Defense, for
legislative affairs, and is now a consultant to the Depart-
ment of Defense. Dee is a fine French cook who gives
cooking lessons in her home; she also is active in the
covenant group ministry of the church and gives parties
(seven course dinners!) for half the world as it passes
through Washington. But in spite of their full schedules,
Dee and Bill give Christ, their marriage, and their family
highest priority. Each Wednesday night, barring a
national crisis, they have their "quality time." Dee prepares one of their favorite French meals, sets a beautiful,
candlelit table in their bedroom, and when Bill comes
home they close the door. Wednesday night is theirs—
no children, no phone calls (except emergencies), and
no interruptions. What they do after dinner—well, who
knows? Whatever it is, it nurtures them and their relationship—and it shows.

Another couple we love and admire greatly are Mary
Jane and John Dellenback. Somehow I always think of
them as a team. The way they pull together, honoring
one another's interests, has given their marriage

relationship a deep sense of oneness and romance.

"A big part of the excitement in our relationship comes from our support of each other," Mary Jane says. "John has encouraged me to become part of his professional life. Traveling with him, as director of the Peace Corps and now as President of the Christian College Coalition, and watching the empathetic way he deals with people and dispatches problems gives me a tremendous surge of pride. He says I've helped him become more skilled in dealing with people, and he has helped me become a more organized, careful thinker. He is the one who urged me to return to school and finish my degree. And he's proud of my accomplishment! My field of interest isn't his, but he listens and learns something of what is exciting me intellectually at the time."

Then Mary Jane remembered something and laughed. "Yes, and he was quick to point out, when we discussed this subject, that we aren't all *that* intellectual in our interest in each other! We just plain, physically, like to be together. We enjoy traveling together, playing tennis together, visiting museums together. We have a lot of fun."

Gene and Jeanine Arnold are another couple alive to one another! Married since she was eighteen and he was nineteen, they have just celebrated their twenty-fifth anniversary, and they still become radiant in each other's presence.

"It's not that we never fuss," Jeanine says. "We fuss fast and get over it fast, and the experience cleanses us of petty grievances. Then we're free to give ourselves wholeheartedly again."

These two have many gifts in their marriage, but there is a special one that Louis and I call the gift of "anointing."

In the New Testament there is a touching scene in which Mary Magdalene anoints Jesus' feet with expensive ointment. Her gesture was more than a generous expression—it was downright extravagant—and the disciples reacted as many of us would to such an act. They reprimanded her, saying, "Why, that nard could have been sold for 200 denarii and given to the poor."

But, as Mary threw practicality to the winds in a bold expression of affection, Jesus affirmed her! His response gave love permission to "anoint" with costly gifts. It is something many of us cannot do often; yet when it is done sincerely, rather than as a sad effort to buy someone's love, it can be a real boon to romance. Our friends, Gene and Jeanine, have learned to anoint one another with exactly that result.

Early in their marriage, Gene, a young Marine, was sent to Korea. Jeanine was pregnant when he left, and their baby, Jennifer, was four months old by the time he returned. On Gene's small sergeant's salary things were tight financially, yet every month, on the date of their marriage, flowers arrived at their home back in the States. The bouquets became a tender link of two hearts whose marriage was also new and tender. Of course, they couldn't afford it, but the "anointing" bonded their relationship with thoughtful bursts of affection that continue to this day.

It is difficult for me to describe where Louie and I are in respect to keeping our romance alive. In fact, this chapter has been hard to write because I've become painfully, yet gratefully, aware of how good God has been to us in our relationship, and how little we sometimes give Him to work with. True, we keep our Thursday nights for each other, but sometimes we are just too tired to do anything but go to bed, a respite for us both, certainly, but not always "quality time." There are pressures and crises in the ministry, even on Thursday, and we sometimes lose our one night a week altogether. I remember one period in our last church when emergencies came in unrelenting waves. It was an incredible time of tragic teenage deaths, community trauma with the church involved, as it should be, at the very core. After many weeks of little rest and no time alone together, the strain took a toll on our relationship. When the calm finally came, as it always does eventually, I called Louie's secretary and asked her to put me down on his schedule for lunch the first day he had a free noon hour. She wrote "Business Lunch" in his appointment book and then added the address of one of our favorite restaurants.

I still remember the look of surprise on Louie's face as he walked into the restaurant that day and found me waiting at a table for two. It was a very romantic meeting. Louie was tender, I shed a few tears, and, fortunately, the restaurant was not very crowded. It was a time of getting back in step, of agreeing to resist the pressures that could keep us apart.

Perhaps, though, it is right for us to yield to these pressures and needs of others occasionally, even if it means missing those special times of recreation together. Yet when we do, it is also right, and *necessary*, to set up another business lunch, or a dinner, or a weekend out of town so that we can be tender and weepy or confronting, or whatever we *must* be in order to feel that we are walking hand in hand again. I guess what I'm saying is, we *are* committed to the need for "quality time" together, but we don't adhere to it rigidly. We get it—somehow, someway—because we need it and even more significantly, we *want* it.

Neither are we anointers, like Gene and Jeanine. Our gifts have been affirming notes pinned on pillows or left on desks. Flowers are not from the florist, but picked by Louie along the road as he jogs in the morning. When it comes to costly gifts, we are both very practical. We always seem to be saving for some purpose or project. So when birthdays or anniversaries come along, our gift is usually a reminder to one another that we are "saving up." With all four children in college or graduate school I don't need to tell you what we are "saving up" for!

What works for one couple will not automatically work for another. Like so many parts of marriage, romance must be custom-made. And yet, in spite of the things we haven't done, God has blessed us with a love that is alive . . . with a sense of romance that keeps us feeling special to each other.

When I asked Louie what was to him the most romantic thing we did together, without hesitation he said, "Backpacking in the high country." Now, bear in mind, we are at our grubbiest at that time—no perfume, candlelight, or soft music—but there *is* a feeling of partnership, a working together, a sharing of both the hardships and the exquisite beauty of the experience, and a stillness that is most romantic to both of us.

One of our special friends in California hates any kind of camping, and I can just hear her saying, "Well, my dear, to each his own." How true!

Romance is not made of shivers and tingles, in spite of what the movies may tell us! Romance is not even what we do or don't do. Doing the right things may embellish a relationship, but basically romance is an attitude. It is a man and woman being alive to one another, not taking one another for granted. It is appreciation expressed in love. It is tenderness in the little things. It is an atmosphere, a look that speaks more eloquently than words, a squeeze of the hand as you pass each other in a crowded room, a pat on the head or the shoulder for no particular reason. Romance is an element of fascination and delight that culminates in a deep desire to experience all of life with the one we love.

Romance helps make marriage the triumph it can be— a triumph that is both a gift from God, and one that "takes *some* doing."

10 Maturity:
A Love for All Seasons

by Coke

I am a some-day jogger—some days I do, and some (most!) days I don't. Today was one of my "do" days, and it felt so good it almost convinced me I should jog every day. We have had an unusually mild and lingering fall in Washington this year, the kind that draws one outdoors and makes even jogging a joy. However, one of these days the season will change. We can count on that. Winter will arrive, and I will be very content to jog through the upstairs hall, or even in place by the side of our bed.

Yes, winter will come, and that is good. There is a rhythm, a dependability, about the seasons that brings a sense of well-being to me. Something in the cycle says, "This is natural; this is right, as it should be." And as it is with the seasons of a year, so it is with the seasons of life, specifically married life. Each season has its own purpose, its own beauty, its dark days and its bright days. Each season is meant to be lived fully, without wishing for one that is past or reaching for one that lies ahead. For when we are too obsessed with yesterday and too anxious about tomorrow, it robs us of today.

Recently I was talking to someone who was researching an article on women. The interviewer asked me, "Aren't you sorry that you gave up all those early years? First you were an actress, and now you are writing—but in between there were so many lost years when all you did was raise a family."

Lost? Was she kidding? I didn't have to consider my answer for a moment!

"No, I'm *not* sorry!" I said. "Those were great years, and I wouldn't have missed them for anything. That was a season of my life—one I enjoyed to the fullest." I meant every word.

Married life does have its seasons, and through them all we are constantly adapting and changing. Goethe wrote: "To live is to adapt." And speaking specifically about marriage, Paul Tournier said:

When God said, 'it is not good that man should be alone,' He intended, by giving him a partner quite different from himself, to force him to face up to a difficult process of mutual adaptation (*The Seasons of Life*, John Knox Press, pp. 29-30).

This "mutual adaptation" is a process involving constant change and it means as husbands and wives we will be working on our relationships until the day we die. And as *we* change, the demands on our time and energies change. New gifts emerge, familiar ones diminish. And this is all part of the cycle, part of the good plan of God.

Being aware that there are seasons, and that one season doesn't last forever, helps a person to live fully in the *now* of life. It helps a person to appreciate the challenge and beauty of today, to celebrate the temporary. At the same time, it provides patience for the difficult times.

For instance, in the season of early marriage, when children are little and parents are up much of the night, sometimes every night for weeks or months, it helps to know that this will not always be their lifestyle. So during the years when the children need their physical presence, parents can give themselves to those demands without resistance, knowing that it will end all too soon.

With four babies under the age of five, I was housebound for years. I remember my mother-in-law assuring me when she visited us that although "No one is more tired than a young mother, this, too, would pass." She was a great help to me. When she told me that she used to fall asleep as she put her four children to bed at night, I smiled because the same thing was happening to me. But I could see that Mother Evans had made it through those years and was, in fact, radiantly enjoying a new season in her life.

Yes, the early marriage years are full of hard work and production—the building of a career and a home. If the husband is the chief wage earner he may have to put aside some of his favorite pasttimes and interests in order to develop those that are important to his work. Building a career consumes much of a man's time and energy at this time of life, but he also has a new life partner. And if a couple has children, they face the challenge of being parents. These relationships deserve "prime time" as much as the career.

When the children are young, a mother needs to give much of herself to them. But that doesn't mean she should leave her husband out of it all! It is the task of *both* parents to raise and care for their children, to fill the emotional baskets of each child. It is their joint responsibility to make sure each one has the love, time, and commitment he or she needs to live life fully. Together, it is hoped they will share life in a way that is so honest and real it will earn them the right to share the riches of Christ with their children in this season of their lives. Giving our children the love and commitment they need is *good*. Orienting our total lives around them is not. There is a lack of health and wholeness in a totally child-oriented home. Dr. Alfred A. Nesser, of Emory University School of Medicine in Atlanta, Georgia, says:

> Perhaps the most significant element in the dissolution of long-standing marriages is a consequence of living in the century of the child (Quoted by J. Allan Petersen in "Partnership before Parenthood," *The Marriage Affair*, Tyndale, p. 121).

Children feel secure when they know their parents love each other. A couple's commitment to each other assures their children that they are part of a strong, loving, and enduring relationship. And it is a relationship that frees, for as the children grow, they are not bound by it. When the home does not rotate solely around the children, the burden of the parents' happiness does not rest on their shoulders. Nor does the home fall apart when the children leave. And so in this early season of marriage, a husband and wife should give their children all that is rightfully theirs; yet they must know that each comes first in the other's affections. "Mommy" and "Daddy" they may be to their children, but, one hopes, not to each other! Marriage begins with a man and a woman and ends the same way. A couple who are partners first, then parents, will not be neglecting their children. They will be nourishing them. They also will be building a strong basis for the seasons yet to come in their lives together.

With such a heavy emphasis on production and work in the early years, a marriage needs a little "theology of play" to balance the relationship. "The family that prays together stays together" is also true when you substitute "plays" for "prays." In fact, if it's all "pray" and no "play," there could be trouble ahead.

Some couples, because of their backgrounds, are naturals at play. Others have to work at it until it becomes natural for them. Sometimes one member of the team is better at play than the other. In our marriage, Louie has the gift of play, and at one point many years ago I had to ask him to teach me. I had worked from the time I was twelve, at full-time summer jobs and part-time jobs during the school year. What I earned was not much, but my mother worked so hard to provide for us that the little I did earn was appreciated. That felt good, and somewhere along the line I became a bit of a workaholic. Louie, on the other hand, had a more carefree childhood, not without responsibilities, but with lots of time and space for play. He also had a brother and two sisters close to his age who were ready-made playmates, whereas I was an only child. Ever since I have known my husband I have been fascinated with his stories of the family trips, the fun, the neighborhood boys and girls, and the mischief they got into together. Those early years served Louie well, for today if he has a free hour, he knows how to use it for fun. He has literally taken me by the hand to show me the way.

When we were first married Louie took me backpacking into the High Sierra of California. Our packs were homemade, our gear the simplest possible, but what a great time we had! I wasn't "taught" to love the high country—I "caught" it, and have had a strong case of mountain fever ever since. I like creature comforts when I'm down off the mountain, and I've been known to smuggle whatever creature comforts I could squeeze into our packs. But the lack of them cannot keep me from the high places. This is a gift I would never have found on my own, a gift Louie brought to our marriage and to our family life.

Louie also taught me to leave a stack of dishes in the sink whenever the rest of the family was ready to take off for a good time. How many times he had to say,

"Come on, Cokie, if we don't leave now, we'll miss the beginning of the game." The first few times he did it, he almost had to pull me away from the sink, but with practice it has become easier for me. Besides, I've learned that if I insist on a perfect kitchen, I'll miss more than the "beginning"—I'll miss the fun!

I'm surprised that so many people lack the capacity for fun and leisure. Perhaps, like me, they need someone to care enough to teach them. Learning to play is an investment, not only in the present, but in the future seasons as well.

Letting Go

When a friend called me recently to tell me, tearfully, that her youngest child had just gone off to college, I thought I understood. "Oh, Sally, you're sad," I said.

But before I could say another word, she interrupted me with, "Sad? Who said anything about being sad? I'm crying because I'm so happy!" Ah, yes, a new season in her life was just beginning. Sally had been happy as a mother with a very full nest (six children), and now she was excited about stepping into a new season—one that included a very interesting, creative career for her.

Not all of us feel the way Sally does. Some of us are afraid, and I can understand. Being at home with a family, demanding as it is, is like being in a comfortable, warm nest. We are familiar with its needs, and from our vantage point the world outside appears to be bristling with responsibilities we feel we may not be able to handle. And so some of us hold back, letting our gifts for this season go undiscovered. Perhaps, because it gives us a feeling of protection, we cling to a submissive role, encouraging our husbands to assume responsibility for our lives.

Protection? From what? From another of God's rich seasons? We do not have to be afraid. Remember we are created to grow, to mature, to adapt. This season of midlife is absolutely bursting with opportunities. I am so excited as I see the potential for growth in my own life—and see evidence of new stirrings in the lives of women all around me.

Many of my friends, especially those who married early, are going back to school. One woman is going to school at night, taking one course at a time. Another is going to the same university her son attends; they wave to each other in the halls. These women are not resisting the middle years. They are excitedly preparing for them. Others are doing beautiful new ministries in the church or community.

A new season means new doors opened. Ruell Howe is right in calling the middle years "The *Creative* Years."

They are also the years of relinquishment. Now we must let go of our children. Someone has said parents are those who give and give, and one day must give away. And we *must*, or we choke to death something we had hoped to keep alive. As partners, we must remind one another that love is not a stranglehold, but a voluntary embrace.

And so our children will leave us. Hopefully they will become independent people and find God's place for them in the world. For some parents this transition is easy, and natural. For others, it is a traumatic loss. When a husband and wife find themselves alone in their home for the first time in many years, that's a new season. If they have kept their love alive, it will be a good season, for the real quality of a relationship is determined by what is left after the children are gone.

Letting go means trusting God. It means allowing God to surprise you with joy as you round the corner, leaning into a new season of life.

New Relationship
Louie and I are certainly "leaning " these days. We are alone in our house for the first time in 25 years, and

loving it. Of course, our children come and go, as do guests, and we thoroughly enjoy them when they do. But to be truthful, the times when we are truly alone, just the two of us, are times we cherish increasingly. God has surprised us with a lovely sense of balance at this time in our lives, something we did not anticipate. We find that we are free to enjoy one another in a new way. We have been married long enough to know better how to do it—old enough to have learned ways of pleasing one another, and young enough to have the energy to carry it off. It's a really wonderful time in our lives together.

Yet we are not always together when we are alone, nor do we have to be. Louie has his work. I have mine. Our lives intertwine, overlap; sometimes we are together, sometimes we are apart. But always there is a sense of moving together to the same music.

I find I identify so much in this season with the words of Anne Morrow Lindberg as she wrote in my favorite *Gift from the Sea.*

A good relationship has a pattern like a dance and is built on some of the same rules. The partners do not need to hold on tightly, because they move confidently in the same pattern, intricate but gay and swift and free, like a country dance of Mozart's. To touch heavily would be to arrest the pattern and freeze the movement, to check the endlessly changing beauty of its unfolding. There is no place here for the possessive clutch, the clinging arm, the heavy hand; only the barest touch in passing. Now arm in arm, now face to face, now back to back—it does not matter which. Because they know they are partners moving to the same rhythm, creating a pattern together, and being invisibly nourished by it (Vintage Books, p. 104).

Simplify

Another aspect of the middle years that we find very rich is the stimulus it has given us to simplify our lives. With the children all away at school, we no longer needed or desired the big house with the big yard. Neither did we need multiple cars. So we made a decision to begin relinquishing possessions. First, we sold the house and moved into a much smaller row house in the middle of the city; it's something we had dreamed of doing for years. Then, simply by cooperating in terms of our schedules, and sometimes using the metro system to get around town, we were able to cut back to one car. Numerous other "things" were jettisoned in the move; passed on to others, recycled, sold. All in all, it was a tremendously freeing process. We felt liberated!

Now what we have done in the area of possessions, we would like to do in the rest of life. We would like to simplify goals and activities; concentrate more on quality than on quantity. But this will be more difficult for us than shedding material acquisitions. We are only just beginning, and have a *long* way to go!

New Gifts

Jung refers to us middle-agers as "the natural motors of existence." If that is true, perhaps now is the time to decelerate the motors just a bit and prepare for the future. If we haven't done it before, we need to simplify and slow down enough to see people more clearly, establish deeper relationships, explore new opportunities to serve and to love. These are the things we can take with us into retirement and beyond. For love is the one thing that goes from season to season, and from this life into the next.

Counselors often talk about the struggle that can accompany the later years when couples have not worked on their relationship in the early and middle seasons. Retirement, they say, can be a very critical period. A wife can become "prickly" about the presence of her unemployed, unoccupied husband who is likely to want *her* to fill the gap left by the absence of his work. Their home is apt to be filled with grumbling, as the wife feels she has to give up her plans for a husband she doesn't know what to do with.

Paul Tournier describes this as a time when couples "realize all at once that they have been living side by side, but have long since ceased being partners."

He goes on: "Blessed are they if they can get through this critical stage, and begin to rebuild, now that they have time, a mutual relationship which they have been gravely neglecting" (*Learn to Grow Old*, Harper & Row, p. 94).

An older friend has said to me, "Coke, you young people [and by that she means us middle-agers] ought to work on your dispositions and relationships because when you are old, you will be just the same—only more so." How true! Charlie Brown's friend Lucy would agree: "The crabby little girls of today," she shouts, "are the crabby old women of tomorrow!"

When my friend urges us to work on ourselves, she really means that we should let God work *in* us. He is our best therapist. He is the one who can straighten out the funny little kinks in our characters and smooth some of these wrinkles in our dispositions. If we are willing to change, and choose to change, He will help us.

Yes, the middle years are good years. They offer a couple greater opportunity for their lives to overlap, the challenge to let their children go and to enjoy them in a totally new relationship, to discover and use new gifts, to simplify and grow in their inner lives. And if they are wise, to prepare for the years to come.

And after that? I must admit, having not yet experienced this later season of married life, I feel at a disadvantage. Certainly there is nothing I can say that would be personal or authoritative. And yet, there are people I know and love who are there right now. I have watched, and I have listened, and because of what I have seen and heard and felt from them, I am a believer in the goodness of *this* season of marriage as much as any other perhaps even more. For when a relationship between a man and wife has been a living, growing organism, will not the passing of seasons make it *more* so, rather than less?

Paul Tournier says:

As one grows old one generally experiences the need for a more restricted but deeper intimacy. This need is fulfilled in the case of a couple who are happy together in the incomparable blessing of growing old together (*Learn to Grow Old*, p. 93).

I think he is right. For I have seen the hands reach out, the tender, knowing pats when they thought no one was watching, and the looks that belied the notion that beyond a certain age people are "just too old to care about such things."

And I have heard their words of affirmation for this season of their life and love. My friend Helen Johns said as she entered her seventieth year, "George and I have never been happier. Life has never been so good." Seeing the look on her face and knowing the quality of life they had together, I believed! Of course, the *joy* of growing old together is the fruit of a lifetime of living, loving, and working through the tough times. This later season depends so much on what has been lived before.

And in this season, as in every other, there are tears as well as happiness. That is life. A couple coming to the later years together walk daily with the possibility of illness, death, and bereavement.

But even the experience of caring for one another, holding hands as you approach the shadowed valley, can be rich and beautiful. I am indebted to Ruth Bell

Graham for this vignette from her parents' lives:

During his last year, Daddy served as Moderator of the Southern Presbyterian Church. Mother had had a stroke several years before which had left her confined to a wheelchair, with her speech slightly affected. Frequently Daddy was up at four in the morning to have his Bible study and time of prayer so he could devote the rest of his day to Mother.

I stood by to help in any way I could, often taking the evening meal down to them and bringing Mother up to stay with me when Daddy would have to be gone for several days.

One morning when I dropped by to see how they were, I found Daddy on his knees in front of Mother, helping her put on her stockings.

Daddy had reached the point where he got up and down with difficulty. He, who had been an athlete in his younger days, and had always kept himself in top physical shape, now found himself with a painfully ulcerated toe that refused to heal due to the fact that he was a borderline diabetic and had lost circulation in his left leg.

He glanced up at me over his glasses, giving me his usual broad smile of welcome.

"You know," he said, returning to Mother's stocking, "these are the happiest days of our lives. Caring for your mother is the greatest privilege of my life."

And the nice things was, he meant it (*It's My Turn,* Ruth Bell Graham, Revell, pp. 177-8).

I do love that story about Dr. and Mrs. Bell. Ruth described their relationship as "Long Term Romance," lovers to the end. And why not? Love in the later season can be deep and steady, and certainly less traumatic than early love. Someone has said that love in the last years seems *more clearly from God; full of the "flavor of eternity."* Though this seaon lies ahead of us, I believe in my heart this must be true. For the Bible (Eph. 5) tells us that marriage is modeled after the relationship our Lord has with the church. When *that* much love is involved, surely time will not tarnish the brightness, or lower the worth of the relationship. Rather, time will only deepen the love and strengthen the ties, even as it adds the richness and flavor of eternity.

What a wonderful promise we have as we give ourselves without reservation to LIFE'S boldest commitments. First, our commitment to Jesus Christ as Saviour and Lord of all life, and then to one another "as long as we both shall live." Both these commitments require submission, courage, sacrifice, and work. Of course! But they also yield fulfillment and joy—more than tongue can tell.

Thank You, God, for creating marriage, and for making it so very, very good!